THE
SONNETS
TO
ORPHEUS
RAINER
MARIA RILKE

Translated,
with an introduction and notes,

by Stephen Mitchell

A TOUCHSTONE BOOK
Published by Simon & Schuster, Inc.
NEW YORK

First Touchstone Edition, 1986

Published by Simon & Schuster, Inc.
Simon & Schuster Building
Rockefeller Center
1230 Avenue of the Americas
New York, New York 10020

TOUCHSTONE and colophon are registered trademarks of Simon & Schuster, Inc.

A number of these translations first appeared, some in earlier versions,
in The Selected Poetry of Rainer Maria Rilke, *edited and translated*
by Stephen Mitchell. Copyright © 1982 by Stephen Mitchell. Reprinted
by permission of Random House, Inc.

Designed by Edith Fowler

Manufactured in the United States of America

10 9 8 7 6 5 4 3 2 1
10 9 8 7 6 5 4 3 2 Pbk.

Library of Congress Cataloging in Publication Data

Rilke, Rainer Maria, 1875–1926.
    The sonnets to Orpheus.

    Translation of: Die Sonette an Orpheus.
    Bibliography: p.
    I. Mitchell, Stephen. II. Title.
PT2635.I65S613 1985   831'.912   85-14399
ISBN: 0-671-55708-4
ISBN: 0-671-61773-7 Pbk.

The illustration on page 2 reproduces a pen-and-ink drawing of
Orpheus (c. 1500) by Cima da Conegliano. A similar reproduction
hung above Rilke's desk at Muzot and helped inspire The Sonnets to
Orpheus.

CONTENTS

INTRODUCTION

I

The great poets disappear into their works. In this they resemble the great sages, who wake up one day to the fact that they are completely transparent. "I'm nobody. Who are you?"

Rilke's life was anything but simple; yet if we step back from the details, we can see that it has an unusually clear pattern to it. All its byways lead to the supreme fulfillment in which *The Sonnets to Orpheus* were written.

As early as 1906, contemplating his face, Rilke felt "as though, from far off, with scattered Things, / a serious, true work were being planned." The beginning of that work was given to him six years later at Duino. It is a famous scene: Rilke walking outside the castle in the January sunlight, trying to clear his mind for a business letter, with a fierce north wind blowing across the Adriatic Sea, when all at once, from a place neither inside nor outside, a voice spoke the first lines of the first Elegy. He was given, as well, a sense that this poem was to be his own justification. Even when the voice became sporadic and, after 1915, ceased altogether, with only four Elegies completed, the certainty of his task remained. It would be a long, difficult lesson in patience.

When life occurs at this level of intensity, biography turns into myth. The myth here resembles that of Psyche and Eros. The god appears, then is gone; and the soul, distraught, must spend seven years wandering in his traces. Finally, she arrives. The god enters, she is caught up in a fulfillment beyond her most extravagant hope. After this, a happy ending seems unnecessary.

Rilke wandered from city to city during and after the War, holding to his certainty and his despair. When at last, at the Château de Muzot, he found the protected solitude he needed in order to plunge back into himself, he had no suspicion that another great work would arise with the Elegies, as their prelude and complement. He settled in, gathering momentum by reading a French prose version of Ovid's *Metamorphoses*, that graceful hodgepodge of dissolved limitations. Then, later in 1921, his lover happened upon a postcard reproduction of an Italian Renaissance drawing. It depicted Orpheus sitting under a tree, playing for the assembled animals (two rabbits, two deer, and a large bird), and before she left Muzot she tacked it to the wall opposite Rilke's desk. The other catalyst was the death of Vera Knoop, the nineteen-year-old daughter of Dutch friends. Rilke barely knew her, but he was profoundly shaken by the news. The very slightness of the actual relationship made her image all the more archetypal.

On February 2, he disappeared into the god. It was "a hurricane in the spirit." For days and nights at a time he stayed in his upstairs room, pacing back and forth, "howling unbelievably vast commands and receiving signals from cosmic space and booming out to them my immense salvos of welcome." By February 23, he was left with six more Elegies, "The Young Workman's Letter," four shorter poems, and sixty-four Sonnets.

This is surely the most astonishing burst of inspiration in the history of literature. Inspiration, because it seems fundamentally different from what other modern poets, even the greatest ones, have known as the process of writing, with all its rawness and groping toward the genuine. There was nothing tentative here. These poems were born perfect; hardly a single word needed to be changed. The whole experience seems to have taken place at an archaic level of consciousness, where the poet is literally the god's or Muse's scribe. We are in the presence of something so intensely real that all our rational categories are useless. Who can respond to it without a shudder of awe?

Such fulfillment, in love or in art, may be excruciatingly difficult to achieve; but we know it is possible. We can feel it resonating from a true marriage. We can see it in the poise of a bodhisattva. And it shines forth, "an incandescence of the intelligence," from a poem that completely accomplishes the poet's intent. Whatever else *The Sonnets to Orpheus* are about, they breathe with the freedom and joy of their creation. They are already their own myth.

II

Why do the inner animals of the first Sonnet, the creatures made of silence, find themselves drawn to the archetypal poet and mysteriously completed in his words? It is not just an esthetic experience for them. The "poetry" is unimportant, and they too dislike it.

Orpheus is a symbol of absolute connection. Perceiving the world without desire, he realizes that, moment by moment, the whole universe is transformed, with all its particular, ungraspable forms. Because he can let go, he is free. He willingly steps into the transforming flame and enters the Double Realm, a mode of being in which all the ordinary human dichotomies (life / death, good / evil) are reconciled in an infinite wholeness.

As Meister Eckhart says of the eternal birth of God, "If it does not occur in me, how can it help me? Everything depends on that." Orpheus is our own inner poet. He is not singing pretty wish-fulfillments. He is singing the truth. That is what draws us, with the enchanted animals, to cluster around him.

How many readers today, how many poets, consider poetry as a spiritual practice? But when we take it seriously enough, the poem becomes transparent, becomes the world illuminated. *Gesang ist Dasein*: through song we can completely be here; or, as Novalis puts it, "The more poetic, the more real." In the space where Orpheus lives, there can be no distinction between beauty and truth, or between psychology and theology. There are no concepts, no crossroads in the heart; instead, pure harmony. We have to be it, with all our dissonances, before we can hear it. It is in that sense, I think, that the poem reads *us,* and that the supreme passages of the supreme poets require our deepest assent. They are mirrors; assent means recognition.

The complement to Orpheus, and the second focal point around which the Sonnets elliptically move, is the young woman (alias Vera, alias Eurydice) who appears in I,2, resurfacing four times afterward in the loveliest and most tactful way. She represents absolute receptivity and is a figure as essential for Rilke as for Vermeer, our other great poet of the anima. When she falls (or, more exactly, rises) asleep in the poet's ear, she returns into the vivid being at the core of us. We may find it strange, perhaps shocking, to consider sleep as a truer state of awareness than the waking mind. But in the Upanishads, for example, it is seen as the closest possible analogy to Godhead: "When man is fast asleep, at peace with himself, happy, without a dream, then that is Self. That is the unalarmed, immortal Spirit." Like the rose which Rilke later chose for his epitaph, this inner woman is pure Self, the delight of being nobody under so many eyelids.

Orpheus has followed her into the root. Because he is forever dead in her, he can reappear in utter acceptance of everything that is alive and earthly. Have there ever been poems so radiant with sensuous experience? The taste of an apple, a horse galloping across a meadow, a flower opening at dawn—all are so intensely present in their ephemeral beauty that outer turns into inner, sense into spirit. Orpheus's transfigured body is a return to the simplest human experiences of seeing and breathing, beyond thought: the huge, vibrant, dangerous world that every child lives in. Though it is transcendence, it leaves nothing behind. It is pure precisely because it goes nowhere.

By the end of the book, Rilke is no longer addressing Orpheus. He has become Orpheus, and can speak to his personal self from the center of the universe. The cycle is completed. Life resolves in a single breath, and the tree of song that sprang up in the first line of the first Sonnet is transformed into the serene, rooted *I am* that is the Sonnets' last word, the word uttered at every moment by each particular form, and also the name of God.

III

In mid-November, when I had almost finished this translation, I was introduced to the great German-born Buddhist scholar Lama Govinda. For a long time I had wanted to ask him about his strange connection with Novalis; and now, thinking about Orpheus, I hoped to gain an insight into the mantric power of language: its ability, literal and symbolic, to move animals, rocks, and trees.

As it happened, we talked mostly about Rilke. I was touched that someone who had spent much of his life in Tibet, immersed in silence, could feel such reverence for the words of a poet. (Another Buddhist teacher once told me, "Of course, poetry itself is delusion. In that case, long live delusion!") He was a small man, well into his eighties, very frail and very alert in his wheelchair; with his bright-yellow silk Chinese jacket, dark-red Tibetan robe, and German accent, he seemed the embodiment of intercultural harmony. For most of the conversation, a large cat lay half-dozing on his lap, its right paw extended onto his left arm in a gesture of extreme indulgence.

Lama Govinda died on January 14, and I was asked to read

Sonnet II,29 at his funeral. I had never thought of it as a death poem. But it is that too. Ahead of all parting. Many friends and students had come to say goodbye, and after the ceremony we were all invited to offer incense. A recent photo of him, eyes glittering with amusement, stood beside the incense bowl on the altar. He seemed to be enjoying all the fuss.

While I read, feeling the poem expand beyond my love for it, into the darkness of the meditation hall—first Rilke's dense, quietly gorgeous music, then the looser rhythms and off-rhymes of my American English—I had been aware of an unusually deep attention in the audience. Afterward, Vicki Chang and I stood for a while in the parking lot of Zen Center's farm. There was a clear, starry sky and a wind passing through the eucalyptus trees. I asked her what that quality of attention had been. She said, "They were listening like deer in the forest. As if their lives depended on it."

Berkeley
February 24, 1985

THE SONNETS TO ORPHEUS

*Written as a grave-monument
for Vera Ouckama Knoop*

Château de Muzot, February 1922

FIRST PART

1

Da stieg ein Baum. O reine Übersteigung!
O Orpheus singt! O hoher Baum im Ohr!
Und alles schwieg. Doch selbst in der Verschweigung
ging neuer Anfang, Wink und Wandlung vor.

Tiere aus Stille drangen aus dem klaren
gelösten Wald von Lager und Genist;
und da ergab sich, daß sie nicht aus List
und nicht aus Angst in sich so leise waren,

sondern aus Hören. Brüllen, Schrei, Geröhr
schien klein in ihren Herzen. Und wo eben
kaum eine Hütte war, dies zu empfangen,

ein Unterschlupf aus dunkelstem Verlangen
mit einem Zugang, dessen Pfosten beben,—
da schufst du ihnen Tempel im Gehör.

1

A tree ascended there. Oh pure transcendence!
Oh Orpheus sings! Oh tall tree in the ear!
And all things hushed. Yet even in that silence
a new beginning, beckoning, change appeared.

Creatures of stillness crowded from the bright
unbound forest, out of their lairs and nests;
and it was not from any dullness, not
from fear, that they were so quiet in themselves,

but from just listening. Bellow, roar, shriek
seemed small inside their hearts. And where there had been
at most a makeshift hut to receive the music,

a shelter nailed up out of their darkest longing,
with an entryway that shuddered in the wind—
you built a temple deep inside their hearing.

ll

Und fast ein Mädchen wars und ging hervor
aus diesem einigen Glück von Sang und Leier
und glänzte klar durch ihre Frühlingsschleier
und machte sich ein Bett in meinem Ohr.

Und schlief in mir. Und alles war ihr Schlaf.
Die Bäume, die ich je bewundert, diese
fühlbare Ferne, die gefühlte Wiese
und jedes Staunen, das mich selbst betraf.

Sie schlief die Welt. Singender Gott, wie hast
du sie vollendet, daß sie nicht begehrte,
erst wach zu sein? Sieh, sie erstand und schlief.

Wo ist ihr Tod? O, wirst du dies Motiv
erfinden noch, eh sich dein Lied verzehrte?—
Wo sinkt sie hin aus mir? . . . Ein Mädchen fast. . . .

ll

And it was almost a girl and came to be
out of this single joy of song and lyre
and through her green veils shone forth radiantly
and made herself a bed inside my ear.

And slept there. And her sleep was everything:
the awesome trees, the distances I had felt
so deeply that I could touch them, meadows in spring:
all wonders that had ever seized my heart.

She slept the world. Singing god, how was that first
sleep so perfect that she had no desire
ever to wake? See: she arose and slept.

Where is her death now? Ah, will you discover
this theme before your song consumes itself?—
Where is she vanishing? . . . A girl almost. . . .

III

Ein Gott vermags. Wie aber, sag mir, soll
ein Mann ihm folgen durch die schmale Leier?
Sein Sinn ist Zwiespalt. An der Kreuzung zweier
Herzwege steht kein Tempel für Apoll.

Gesang, wie du ihn lehrst, ist nicht Begehr,
nicht Werbung um ein endlich noch Erreichtes;
Gesang ist Dasein. Für den Gott ein Leichtes.
Wann aber sind wir? Und wann wendet er

an unser Sein die Erde und die Sterne?
Dies ists nicht, Jüngling, daß du liebst, wenn auch
die Stimme dann den Mund dir aufstößt,—lerne

vergessen, daß du aufsangst. Das verrinnt.
In Wahrheit singen, ist ein andrer Hauch.
Ein Hauch um nichts. Ein Wehn im Gott. Ein Wind.

lll

A god can do it. But will you tell me how
a man can enter through the lyre's strings?
Our mind is split. And at the shadowed crossing
of heart-roads, there is no temple for Apollo.

Song, as you have taught it, is not desire,
not wooing any grace that can be achieved;
song is reality. Simple, for a god.
But when can *we* be real? When does he pour

the earth, the stars, into us? Young man,
it is not your loving, even if your mouth
was forced wide open by your own voice—learn

to forget that passionate music. It will end.
True singing is a different breath, about
nothing. A gust inside the god. A wind.

IV

O ihr Zärtlichen, tretet zuweilen
in den Atem, der euch nicht meint,
laßt ihn an eueren Wangen sich teilen,
hinter euch zittert er, wieder vereint.

O ihr Seligen, o ihr Heilen,
die ihr der Anfang der Herzen scheint.
Bogen der Pfeile und Ziele von Pfeilen,
ewiger glänzt euer Lächeln verweint.

Fürchtet euch nicht zu leiden, die Schwere,
gebt sie zurück an der Erde Gewicht;
schwer sind die Berge, schwer sind die Meere.

Selbst die als Kinder ihr pflanztet, die Bäume,
wurden zu schwer längst; ihr trüget sie nicht.
Aber die Lüfte . . . aber die Räume. . . .

IV

O you tender ones, walk now and then
into the breath that blows coldly past.
Upon your cheeks let it tremble and part;
behind you it will tremble together again.

O you blessèd ones, you who are whole,
you who seem the beginning of hearts,
bows for the arrows and arrows' targets—
tear-bright, your lips more eternally smile.

Don't be afraid to suffer; return
that heaviness to the earth's own weight;
heavy are the mountains, heavy the seas.

Even the small trees you planted as children
have long since become too heavy; you could not
carry them now. But the winds . . . But the spaces. . . .

V

Errichtet keinen Denkstein. Laßt die Rose
nur jedes Jahr zu seinen Gunsten blühn.
Denn Orpheus ists. Seine Metamorphose
in dem und dem. Wir sollen uns nicht mühn

um andre Namen. Ein für alle Male
ists Orpheus, wenn es singt. Er kommt und geht.
Ists nicht schon viel, wenn er die Rosenschale
um ein paar Tage manchmal übersteht?

O wie er schwinden muß, daß ihrs begrifft!
Und wenn ihm selbst auch bangte, daß er schwände.
Indem sein Wort das Hiersein übertrifft,

ist er schon dort, wohin ihrs nicht begleitet.
Der Leier Gitter zwängt ihm nicht die Hände.
Und er gehorcht, indem er überschreitet.

V

Erect no gravestone for him. Only this:
let the rose blossom each year for his sake.
For it *is* the god. His metamorphosis
in this and that. We do not need to look

for other names. It is Orpheus once for all
whenever there is song. He comes and goes.
Isn't it enough if sometimes he can dwell
with us a few days longer than a rose?

Though he himself is afraid to disappear,
he *has* to vanish: don't you understand?
The moment his word moves out beyond our life here,

he has gone where you will never find his trace.
The lyre's strings do not constrict his hands.
And it is in overstepping that he obeys.

VI

Ist er ein Hiesiger? Nein, aus beiden
Reichen erwuchs seine weite Natur.
Kundiger böge die Zweige der Weiden,
wer die Wurzeln der Weiden erfuhr.

Geht ihr zu Bette, so laßt auf dem Tische
Brot nicht und Milch nicht; die Toten ziehts—.
Aber er, der Beschwörende, mische
unter der Milde des Augenlids

ihre Erscheinung in alles Geschaute;
und der Zauber von Erdrauch und Raute
sei ihm so wahr wie der klarste Bezug.

Nichts kann das gültige Bild ihm verschlimmern;
sei es aus Gräbern, sei es aus Zimmern,
rühme er Fingerring, Spange und Krug.

VI

Is he someone who dwells in this *single* world? No:
both realms are the source of his earthly power.
He alone who has known the roots of the willow
can bend the willow-branch into a lyre.

Overnight leave no bread on the table
and leave no milk: they draw back the dead—.
But he, the conjuror, may he settle
under the calm of the eye's lowered lid

to mix death into everything seen;
and may the magic of earthsmoke and rue
be as real to him as the clearest connection.

Nothing can trouble the dominance of
the true image. Whether from graves or from rooms,
let him praise finger-ring, bracelet, and jug.

VII

Rühmen, das ists! Ein zum Rühmen Bestellter,
ging er hervor wie das Erz aus des Steins
Schweigen. Sein Herz, o vergängliche Kelter
eines den Menschen unendlichen Weins.

Nie versagt ihm die Stimme am Staube,
wenn ihn das göttliche Beispiel ergreift.
Alles wird Weinberg, alles wird Traube,
in seinem fühlenden Süden gereift.

Nicht in den Grüften der Könige Moder
straft ihm die Rühmung lügen, oder
daß von den Göttern ein Schatten fällt.

Er ist einer der bleibenden Boten,
der noch weit in die Türen der Toten
Schalen mit rühmlichen Früchten hält.

VII

Praising is what matters! He was summoned for that,
and came to us like the ore from a stone's
silence. His mortal heart presses out
a deathless, inexhaustible wine.

Whenever he feels the god's paradigm grip
his throat, the voice does not die in his mouth.
All becomes vineyard, all becomes grape,
ripened on the hills of his sensuous South.

Neither decay in the sepulcher of kings
nor any shadow fallen from the gods
can ever detract from his glorious praising.

For he is a herald who is with us always,
holding far into the doors of the dead
a bowl with ripe fruit worthy of praise.

VIII

Nur im Raum der Rühmung darf die Klage
gehn, die Nymphe des geweinten Quells,
wachend über unserm Niederschlage,
daß er klar sei an demselben Fels,

der die Tore trägt und die Altäre.—
Sieh, um ihre stillen Schultern früht
das Gefühl, daß sie die jüngste wäre
unter den Geschwistern im Gemüt.

Jubel weiß, und Sehnsucht ist geständig,—
nur die Klage lernt noch; mädchenhändig
zählt sie nächtelang das alte Schlimme.

Aber plötzlich, schräg und ungeübt,
hält sie doch ein Sternbild unsrer Stimme
in den Himmel, den ihr Hauch nicht trübt.

VIII

Only in the realm of Praising should Lament
walk, the naiad of the wept-for fountain,
watching over the stream of our complaint,
to keep it clear upon the very stone

that bears the arch of triumph and the altar.—
Look: around her shoulders dawns the bright
sense that she may be the youngest sister
among the deities hidden in our heart.

Joy *knows*, and Longing has accepted—
only Lament still learns; upon her beads,
night after night, she counts the ancient curse.

Yet awkward as she is, she suddenly
lifts a constellation of our voice,
glittering, into the pure nocturnal sky.

IX

Nur wer die Leier schon hob
auch unter Schatten,
darf das unendliche Lob
ahnend erstatten.

Nur wer mit Toten vom Mohn
aß, von dem ihren,
wird nicht den leisesten Ton
wieder verlieren.

Mag auch die Spieglung im Teich
oft uns verschwimmen:
Wisse das Bild.

Erst in dem Doppelbereich
werden die Stimmen
ewig und mild.

IX

Only he whose bright lyre
has sounded in shadows
may, looking onward, restore
his infinite praise.

Only he who has eaten
poppies with the dead
will not lose ever again
the gentlest chord.

Though the image upon the pool
often grows dim:
Know and be still.

Inside the Double World
all voices become
eternally mild.

X

Euch, die ihr nie mein Gefühl verließt,
grüß ich, antikische Sarkophage,
die das fröhliche Wasser römischer Tage
als ein wandelndes Lied durchfließt.

Oder jene so offenen, wie das Aug
eines frohen erwachenden Hirten,
—innen voll Stille und Bienensaug—
denen entzückte Falter entschwirrten;

alle, die man dem Zweifel entreißt,
grüß ich, die wiedergeöffneten Munde,
die schon wußten, was schweigen heißt.

Wissen wirs, Freunde, wissen wirs nicht?
Beides bildet die zögernde Stunde
in dem menschlichen Angesicht.

X

You who are close to my heart always,
I welcome you, ancient coffins of stone,
which the cheerful water of Roman days
still flows through, like a wandering song.

Or those other ones that are open wide
like the eyes of a happily waking shepherd
—with silence and bee-suck nettle inside,
from which ecstatic butterflies flittered;

everything that has been wrestled from doubt
I welcome—the mouths that burst open after
long knowledge of what it is to be mute.

Do we know this, my friends, or don't we know this?
Both are formed by the hesitant hour
in the deep calm of the human face.

XI

Sieh den Himmel. Heißt kein Sternbild ›Reiter‹?
Denn dies ist uns seltsam eingeprägt:
dieser Stolz aus Erde. Und ein Zweiter,
der ihn treibt und hält und den er trägt.

Ist nicht so, gejagt und dann gebändigt,
diese sehnige Natur des Seins?
Weg und Wendung. Doch ein Druck verständigt.
Neue Weite. Und die zwei sind eins.

Aber sind sie's? Oder meinen beide
nicht den Weg, den sie zusammen tun?
Namenlos schon trennt sie Tisch und Weide.

Auch die sternische Verbindung trügt.
Doch uns freue eine Weile nun
der Figur zu glauben. Das genügt.

XI

Look at the sky. Are no two stars called "Rider"?
For this is printed strangely on us here:
this pride of earth. And look, the second figure
who drives and halts it: whom it has to bear.

Aren't we, in our sinewy quintessence,
controlled like this, now raced and now reined in?
Path and turningpoint. Just a touch possesses.
New expanses. And the two are one.

Or *are* they really? Don't both signify
the path they ride together now? But table
and pasture keep them separate, utterly.

Even the starry union is a fraud.
Yet gladly let us trust the valid symbol
for a moment. It is all we need.

XII

Heil dem Geist, der uns verbinden mag;
denn wir leben wahrhaft in Figuren.
Und mit kleinen Schritten gehn die Uhren
neben unserm eigentlichen Tag.

Ohne unsern wahren Platz zu kennen,
handeln wir aus wirklichem Bezug.
Die Antennen fühlen die Antennen,
und die leere Ferne trug . . .

Reine Spannung. O Musik der Kräfte!
Ist nicht durch die läßlichen Geschäfte
jede Störung von dir abgelenkt?

Selbst wenn sich der Bauer sorgt und handelt,
wo die Saat in Sommer sich verwandelt,
reicht er niemals hin. Die Erde schenkt.

XII

Hail to the god who joins us; for through him
arise the symbols where we truly live.
And, with tiny footsteps, the clocks move
separately from our authentic time.

Though we are unaware of our true status,
our actions stem from pure relationship.
Far away, antennas hear antennas
and the empty distances transmit . . .

Pure readiness. Oh unheard starry music!
Isn't your sound protected from all static
by the ordinary business of our days?

In spite of all the farmer's work and worry,
he can't reach down to where the seed is slowly
transmuted into summer. The earth *bestows*.

XIII

Voller Apfel, Birne und Banane,
Stachelbeere . . . Alles dieses spricht
Tod und Leben in den Mund . . . Ich ahne . . .
Lest es einem Kind vom Angesicht,

wenn es sie erschmeckt. Dies kommt von weit.
Wird euch langsam namenlos im Munde?
Wo sonst Worte waren, fließen Funde,
aus dem Fruchtfleisch überrascht befreit.

Wagt zu sagen, was ihr Apfel nennt.
Diese Süße, die sich erst verdichtet,
um, im Schmecken leise aufgerichtet,

klar zu werden, wach und transparent,
doppeldeutig, sonnig, erdig, hiesig—:
O Erfahrung, Fühlung, Freude—, riesig!

XIII

Plump apple, smooth banana, melon, peach,
gooseberry . . . How all this affluence
speaks death and life into the mouth . . . I sense . . .
Observe it from a child's transparent features

while he tastes. This comes from far away.
What miracle is happening in your mouth?
Instead of words, discoveries flow out
from the ripe flesh, astonished to be free.

Dare to say what "apple" truly is.
This sweetness that feels thick, dark, dense at first;
then, exquisitely lifted in your taste,

grows clarified, awake and luminous,
double-meaninged, sunny, earthy, real—:
Oh knowledge, pleasure—inexhaustible.

XIV

Wir gehen um mit Blume, Weinblatt, Frucht.
Sie sprechen nicht die Sprache nur des Jahres.
Aus Dunkel steigt ein buntes Offenbares
und hat vielleicht den Glanz der Eifersucht

der Toten an sich, die die Erde stärken.
Was wissen wir von ihrem Teil an dem?
Es ist seit lange ihre Art, den Lehm
mit ihrem freien Marke zu durchmärken.

Nun fragt sich nur: tun sie es gern? . . .
Drängt diese Frucht, ein Werk von schweren Sklaven,
geballt zu uns empor, zu ihren Herrn?

Sind sie die Herrn, die bei den Wurzeln schlafen,
und gönnen uns aus ihren Überflüssen
dies Zwischending aus stummer Kraft und Küssen?

XIV

We are involved with flower, leaf, and fruit.
They speak not just the language of one year.
From darkness a bright phenomenon appears
and still reflects, perhaps, the jealous glint

of the dead, who fill the earth. How can we know
what part they play within the ancient cycle?
Long since, it has been their job to make the soil
vigorous with the force of their free marrow.

But have they done it willingly? we ask . . .
Does this fruit, formed by heavy slaves, push up
like a clenched fist, to threaten us, their masters?

Or in fact are *they* the masters, as they sleep
beside the roots and grant us, from their riches,
this hybrid Thing of speechless strength and kisses?

XV

Wartet . . . , das schmeckt . . . Schon ists auf der Flucht.
. . . . Wenig Musik nur, ein Stampfen, ein Summen—:
Mädchen, ihr warmen, Mädchen, ihr stummen,
tanzt den Geschmack der erfahrenen Frucht!

Tanzt die Orange. Wer kann sie vergessen,
wie sie, ertrinkend in sich, sich wehrt
wider ihr Süßsein. Ihr habt sie besessen.
Sie hat sich köstlich zu euch bekehrt.

Tanzt die Orange. Die wärmere Landschaft,
werft sie aus euch, daß die reife erstrahle
in Lüften der Heimat! Erglühte, enthüllt

Düfte um Düfte. Schafft die Verwandtschaft
mit der reinen, sich weigernden Schale,
mit dem Saft, der die Glückliche füllt!

———

XV

Wait . . . , that tastes good . . . But already it's gone.
. . . . A few notes of music, a tapping, a faint
hum—: you girls, so warm and so silent,
dance the taste of the fruit you have known!

Dance the orange. Who can forget it,
drowning in itself, how it struggles through
against its own sweetness. You have possessed it.
Deliciously it has converted to you.

Dance the orange. The sunnier landscape—
fling it *from* you, allow it to shine
in the breeze of its homeland! Aglow, peel away

scent after scent. Create your own kinship
with the supple, gently reluctant rind
and the juice that fills it with succulent joy.

XVI

Du, mein Freund, bist einsam, weil. . . .
Wir machen mit Worten und Fingerzeigen
uns allmählich die Welt zu eigen,
vielleicht ihren schwächsten, gefährlichsten Teil.

Wer zeigt mit Fingern auf einen Geruch?—
Doch von den Kräften, die uns bedrohten,
fühlst du viele . . . Du kennst die Toten,
und du erschrickst vor dem Zauberspruch.

Sieh, nun heißt es zusammen ertragen
Stückwerk und Teile, als sei es das Ganze.
Dir helfen, wird schwer sein. Vor allem: pflanze

mich nicht in dein Herz. Ich wüchse zu schnell.
Doch meines Herrn Hand will ich führen und sagen:
Hier. Das ist Esau in seinem Fell.

XVI

You are lonely, my friend, because you are. . . .
We, with a word or a finger-sign,
gradually make the world our own,
though perhaps its weakest, most precarious part.

How can fingers point out a smell?—
Yet of the dark forces that lurk at our side
you feel many . . . You know the dead,
and you shrink away from the magic spell.

Look, we two together must bear
piecework and parts, as if they were
the whole. But be careful. Above all, don't plant

me inside your heart. I'd outgrow you. But I
will guide *my* master's hand and will say:
Here. This is Esau beneath his pelt.

XVII

Zu unterst der Alte, verworrn,
all der Erbauten
Wurzel, verborgener Born,
den sie nie schauten.

Sturmhelm und Jägerhorn,
Spruch von Ergrauten,
Männer im Bruderzorn,
Frauen wie Lauten . . .

Drängender Zweig an Zweig,
nirgends ein freier. . . .
Einer! O steig . . . o steig . . .

Aber sie brechen noch.
Dieser erst oben doch
biegt sich zur Leier.

XVII

At bottom the Ancient One, gnarled
root hidden deep,
origin unbeheld
by those who branched up.

Helmet and horn of hunters,
grandfathers' truths,
men who betrayed their brothers,
women like lutes . . .

Branch upon branch crowds close,
none of them free. . . .
Keep climbing higher . . . higher . . .

Still, though, they break. Yet this
top one bends finally
into a lyre.

XVIII

Hörst du das Neue, Herr,
dröhnen und beben?
Kommen Verkündiger,
die es erheben.

Zwar ist kein Hören heil
in dem Durchtobtsein,
doch der Maschinenteil
will jetzt gelobt sein.

Sieh, die Maschine:
wie sie sich wälzt und rächt
und uns entstellt und schwächt.

Hat sie aus uns auch Kraft,
sie, ohne Leidenschaft,
treibe und diene.

XVIII

Master, do you hear the New
quiver and rumble?
Harbingers step forth who
blare their approval.

Surely no ear is whole
amid this noise,
yet the machine-part still
asks for our praise.

Look, the machine:
rears up and takes revenge,
brings us to crawl and cringe.

Since all its strength is from us,
let it, desireless,
serve and remain.

XIX

Wandelt sich rasch auch die Welt
wie Wolkengestalten,
alles Vollendete fällt
heim zum Uralten.

Über dem Wandel und Gang,
weiter und freier,
währt noch dein Vor-Gesang,
Gott mit der Leier.

Nicht sind die Leiden erkannt,
nicht ist die Liebe gelernt,
und was im Tod uns entfernt,

ist nicht entschleiert.
Einzig das Lied überm Land
heiligt und feiert.

XIX

Though the world keeps changing its form
as fast as a cloud, still
what is accomplished falls home
to the Primeval.

Over the change and the passing,
larger and freer,
soars your eternal song,
god with the lyre.

Never has grief been possessed,
never has love been learned,
and what removes us in death

is not revealed.
Only the song through the land
hallows and heals.

XX

Dir aber, Herr, o was weih ich dir, sag,
der das Ohr den Geschöpfen gelehrt?—
Mein Erinnern an einen Frühlingstag,
seinen Abend, in Rußland—, ein Pferd . . .

Herüber vom Dorf kam der Schimmel allein,
an der vorderen Fessel den Pflock,
um die Nacht auf den Wiesen allein zu sein;
wie schlug seiner Mähne Gelock

an den Hals im Takte des Übermuts,
bei dem grob gehemmten Galopp.
Wie sprangen die Quellen des Rossebluts!

Der fühlte die Weiten, und ob!
Der sang und der hörte—, dein Sagenkreis
war in ihm geschlossen.
                    Sein Bild: ich weih's.

XX

But Master, what gift shall I dedicate to you,
who taught all creatures their ears?
—My thoughts of an evening long ago,
it was springtime, in Russia—a horse . . .

He came bounding from the village, alone, white,
with a hobble attached to one leg,
to stay alone in the fields all night;
how the mane beat against his neck

to the rhythm of his perfect joy, in that hindered
gallop across the meadow.
What leaping went on in his stallion-blood!

He felt the expanses, and oh!
He sang and he heard—your cycle of myths
was completed *in* him.

His image: my gift.

XXI

Frühling ist wiedergekommen. Die Erde
ist wie ein Kind, das Gedichte weiß;
viele, o viele. . . . Für die Beschwerde
langen Lernens bekommt sie den Preis.

Streng war ihr Lehrer. Wir mochten das Weiße
an dem Barte des alten Manns.
Nun, wie das Grüne, das Blaue heiße,
dürfen wir fragen: sie kanns, sie kanns!

Erde, die frei hat, du glückliche, spiele
nun mit den Kindern. Wir wollen dich fangen,
fröhliche Erde. Dem Frohsten gelingts.

O, was der Lehrer sie lehrte, das Viele,
und was gedruckt steht in Wurzeln und langen
schwierigen Stämmen: sie singts, sie singts!

XXI

Spring has returned. The earth resembles
a little girl who has memorized
many poems. . . . For all the trouble
of her long learning, she wins the prize.

Her teacher was strict. We loved the white
in the old man's beard and shaggy eyebrows.
Now, whatever we ask about
the blue and the green, she knows, she knows!

Earth, overjoyed to be out on vacation,
play with the children. We long to catch up,
jubilant Earth. The happiest will win.

What her teacher taught her, the numberless Things,
and what lies hidden in stem and in deep
difficult root, she sings, she sings!

XXII

Wir sind die Treibenden.
Aber den Schritt der Zeit,
nehmt ihn als Kleinigkeit
im immer Bleibenden.

Alles das Eilende
wird schon vorüber sein;
denn das Verweilende
erst weiht uns ein.

Knaben, o werft den Mut
nicht in die Schnelligkeit,
nicht in den Flugversuch.

Alles ist ausgeruht:
Dunkel und Helligkeit,
Blume und Buch.

XXII

We are the driving ones.
Ah, but the step of time:
think of it as a dream
in what forever remains.

All that is hurrying
soon will be over with;
only what lasts can bring
us to the truth.

Young men, don't put your trust
into the trials of flight,
into the hot and quick.

All things already rest:
darkness and morning light,
flower and book.

XXIII

O erst dann, *wenn der Flug*
nicht mehr um seinetwillen
wird in die Himmelstillen
steigen, sich selber genug,

um in lichten Profilen,
als das Gerät, das gelang,
Liebling der Winde zu spielen,
sicher, schwenkend und schlank,—

erst, wenn ein reines Wohin
wachsender Apparate
Knabenstolz überwiegt,

wird, überstürzt von Gewinn,
jener den Fernen Genahte
sein, *was er einsam erfliegt.*

XXIII

Not till the day when flight
no longer for its own sake ascends
into the silent heavens
propelled by its self-conceit,

so that, in luminous outlines,
as the tool that has come to power,
it can float, caressed by the winds,
streamlined, agile, and sure—

not till a pure destination
outweighs the boyish boast
of how much machines can do

will, overwhelmed with gain,
one to whom distance is close
be what alone he flew.

XXIV

Sollen wir unsere uralte Freundschaft, die großen
niemals werbenden Götter, weil sie der harte
Stahl, den wir streng erzogen, nicht kennt, verstoßen
oder sie plötzlich suchen auf einer Karte?

Diese gewaltigen Freunde, die uns die Toten
nehmen, rühren nirgends an unsere Räder.
Unsere Gastmähler haben wir weit—, unsere Bäder,
fortgerückt, und ihre uns lang schon zu langsamen Boten

überholen wir immer. Einsamer nun auf einander
ganz angewiesen, ohne einander zu kennen,
führen wir nicht mehr die Pfade als schöne Mäander,

sondern als Grade. Nur noch in Dampfkesseln brennen
die einstigen Feuer und heben die Hämmer, die immer
größern. Wir aber nehmen an Kraft ab, wie Schwimmer.

XXIV

Shall we reject our primordial friendship, the sublime
unwooing gods, because the steel that we keep
harshly bringing to hardness has never known them—
or shall we suddenly look for them on a map?

All these powerful friends, who withdraw the dead
from the reach of the senses, touch nowhere against our
        wheels.
We have moved our banquets, our baths and our festivals,
far away. And their messengers, long since outstripped by
        our speed,

have vanished. Lonelier now, dependent on one another
utterly, though not knowing one another at all,
we no longer lay out each path as a lovely meander,

but straight ahead. Only in factories do the once-
        consecrate flames still
burn and lift up the always heavier hammers.
We, though, keep losing what small strength we have, like
        swimmers.

XXV

Dich *aber will ich nun,* Dich, *die ich kannte*
wie eine Blume, von der ich den Namen nicht weiß,
noch ein *Mal erinnern und ihnen zeigen, Entwandte,*
schöne Gespielin des unüberwindlichen Schrei's.

Tänzerin erst, die plötzlich, den Körper voll Zögern,
anhielt, als göß man ihr Jungsein in Erz;
trauernd und lauschend—. Da, von den hohen Vermögern
fiel ihr Musik in das veränderte Herz.

Nah war die Krankheit. Schon von den Schatten bemächtigt,
drängte verdunkelt das Blut, doch, wie flüchtig verdächtigt,
trieb es in seinen natürlichen Frühling hervor.

Wieder und wieder, von Dunkel und Sturz unterbrochen,
glänzte es irdisch. Bis es nach schrecklichem Pochen
trat in das trostlos offene Tor.

XXV

But you now, dear girl, whom I loved like a flower whose
      name
I didn't know, you who so early were taken away:
I will once more call up your image and show it to them,
beautiful companion of the unsubduable cry.

Dancer whose body filled with your hesitant fate,
pausing, as though your young flesh had been cast in
      bronze;
grieving and listening—. Then, from the high dominions,
unearthly music fell into your altered heart.

Already possessed by shadows, with illness near,
your blood flowed darkly; yet, though for a moment
      suspicious,
it burst out into the natural pulses of spring.

Again and again interrupted by downfall and darkness,
earthly, it gleamed. Till, after a terrible pounding,
it entered the inconsolably open door.

XXVI

Du aber, Göttlicher, du, bis zuletzt noch Ertöner,
da ihn der Schwarm der verschmähten Mänaden befiel,
hast ihr Geschrei übertönt mit Ordnung, du Schöner,
aus den Zerstörenden stieg dein erbauendes Spiel.

Keine war da, daß sie Haupt dir und Leier zerstör.
Wie sie auch rangen und rasten, und alle die scharfen
Steine, die sie nach deinem Herzen warfen,
wurden zu Sanftem an dir und begabt mit Gehör.

Schließlich zerschlugen sie dich, von der Rache gehetzt,
während dein Klang noch in Löwen und Felsen verweilte
und in den Bäumen und Vögeln. Dort singst du noch jetzt.

O du verlorener Gott! Du unendliche Spur!
Nur weil dich reißend zuletzt die Feindschaft verteilte,
sind wir die Hörenden jetzt und ein Mund der Natur.

XXVI

But you, divine poet, you who sang on till the end
as the swarm of rejected maenads attacked you, shrieking,
you overpowered their noise with harmony, and
from pure destruction arose your transfigured song.

Their hatred could not destroy your head or your lyre,
however they wrestled and raged; and each one of the
          sharp
stones that they hurled, vengeance-crazed, at your heart
softened while it was in mid-flight, enchanted to hear.

At last they killed you and broke you in pieces while
your sound kept lingering on in lions and boulders,
in trees and in birds. There you are singing still.

Oh you lost god! You inexhaustible trace!
Only because you were torn and scattered through Nature
have *we* become hearers now and a rescuing voice.

SECOND PART

1

Atmen, du unsichtbares Gedicht!
Immerfort um das eigne
Sein rein eingetauschter Weltraum. Gegengewicht,
in dem ich mich rhythmisch ereigne.

Einzige Welle, deren
allmähliches Meer ich bin;
sparsamstes du von allen möglichen Meeren,—
Raumgewinn.

Wieviele von diesen Stellen der Räume waren schon
innen in mir. Manche Winde
sind wie mein Sohn.

Erkennst du mich, Luft, du, voll noch einst meiniger Orte?
Du, einmal glatte Rinde,
Rundung und Blatt meiner Worte.

1

Breathing: you invisible poem! Complete
interchange of our own
essence with world-space. You counterweight
in which I rhythmically happen.

Single wave-motion whose
gradual sea I am;
you, most inclusive of all our possible seas—
space grown warm.

How many regions in space have already been
inside me. There are winds that seem like
my wandering son.

Do you recognize me, air, full of places I once absorbed?
You who were the smooth bark,
roundness, and leaf of my words.

ll

*So wie dem Meister manchmal das eilig
nähere Blatt den wirklichen Strich
abnimmt: so nehmen oft Spiegel das heilig
einzige Lächeln der Mädchen in sich,*

*wenn sie den Morgen erproben, allein,—
oder im Glanze der dienenden Lichter.
Und in das Atmen der echten Gesichter,
später, fällt nur ein Widerschein.*

*Was haben Augen einst ins umrußte
lange Verglühn der Kamine geschaut:
Blicke des Lebens, für immer verlorne.*

*Ach, der Erde, wer kennt die Verluste?
Nur, wer mit dennoch preisendem Laut
sänge das Herz, das ins Ganze geborne.*

ll

Just as the master's *genuine* brushstroke
is sometimes caught by a hurried page
that happens to be there: so mirrors will take
into themselves the pure smiling image

of girls as they test the morning, alone—
or under the gleam of devoted candles.
And into their faces, one by one,
later, just a reflection falls.

How much was once gazed into the charred
slow-dying glow of a fireplace:
glances of life, irretrievable.

Who knows what losses the earth has suffered?
One who, with sounds that nonetheless praise,
can sing the heart born into the whole.

III

Spiegel: noch nie hat man wissend beschrieben,
was ihr in euerem Wesen seid.
Ihr, wie mit lauter Löchern von Sieben
erfüllten Zwischenräume der Zeit.

Ihr, noch des leeren Saales Verschwender—,
wenn es dämmert, wie Wälder weit . . .
Und der Lüster geht wie ein Sechzehn-Ender
durch eure Unbetretbarkeit.

Manchmal seid ihr voll Malerei.
Einige scheinen in euch gegangen—,
andere schicktet ihr scheu vorbei.

Aber die Schönste wird bleiben—, bis
drüben in ihre enthaltenen Wangen
eindrang der klare gelöste Narziß.

III

Mirrors: no one has ever known how
to describe what you are in your inmost realm.
As if filled with nothing but sieve-holes, you
fathomless in-between spaces of time.

You prodigals of the empty chamber—
vast as forests, at the close of day . . .
And the chandelier strides like a sixteen-pointer
through your unenterability.

Sometimes you are full of painting. A few
seem to have walked straight into your depths—
others, shyly, you sent on past you.

But the loveliest will stay—until, beyond,
into her all-absorbed cheeks she lets
Narcissus penetrate, bright and unbound.

IV

O dieses ist das Tier, das es nicht giebt.
Sie wußtens nicht und habens jeden Falls
—sein Wandeln, seine Haltung, seinen Hals,
bis in des stillen Blickes Licht—geliebt.

Zwar war es nicht. Doch weil sie's liebten, ward
ein reines Tier. Sie ließen immer Raum.
Und in dem Raume, klar und ausgespart,
erhob es leicht sein Haupt und brauchte kaum

zu sein. Sie nährten es mit keinem Korn,
nur immer mit der Möglichkeit, es sei.
Und die gab solche Stärke an das Tier,

daß es aus sich ein Stirnhorn trieb. Ein Horn.
Zu einer Jungfrau kam es weiß herbei—
und war im Silber-Spiegel und in ihr.

IV

Oh this beast is the one that never was.
They didn't know that; unconcerned, they had
loved its grace, its walk, and how it stood
looking at them calmly, with clear eyes.

It hadn't *been*. But from their love, a pure
beast arose. They always left it room.
And in that heart-space, radiant and bare,
it raised its head and hardly needed to

exist. They fed it, not with any grain,
but always just with the thought that it might be.
And this assurance gave the beast so much power,

it grew a horn upon its brow. One horn.
Afterward it approached a virgin, whitely—
and was, inside the mirror and in her.

V

Blumenmuskel, der der Anemone
Wiesenmorgen nach und nach erschließt,
bis in ihren Schooß das polyphone
Licht der lauten Himmel sich ergießt,

in den stillen Blütenstern gespannter
Muskel des unendlichen Empfangs,
manchmal so von Fülle übermannter,
daß der Ruhewink des Untergangs

kaum vermag die weitzurückgeschnellten
Blätterränder dir zurückzugeben:
du, Entschluß und Kraft von wieviel Welten!

Wir, Gewaltsamen, wir währen länger.
Aber wann, in welchem aller Leben,
sind wir endlich offen und Empfänger?

V

Flower-muscle that slowly opens back
the anemone to another meadow-dawn,
until her womb can feel the polyphonic
light of the sonorous heavens pouring down;

muscle of an infinite acceptance,
stretched within the silent blossom-star,
at times *so* overpowered with abundance
that sunset's signal for repose is bare-

ly able to return your too far hurled-
back petals for the darkness to revive:
you, strength and purpose of how many worlds!

We violent ones remain a little longer.
Ah but *when*, in which of all our lives,
shall we at last be open and receivers?

VI

Rose, du thronende, denen im Altertume
warst du ein Kelch mit einfachem Rand.
Uns *aber bist du die volle zahllose Blume,*
der unerschöpfliche Gegenstand.

In deinem Reichtum scheinst du wie Kleidung um Kleidung
um einen Leib aus nichts als Glanz;
aber dein einzelnes Blatt ist zugleich die Vermeidung
und die Verleugnung jedes Gewands.

Seit Jahrhunderten ruft uns dein Duft
seine süßesten Namen herüber;
plötzlich liegt er wie Ruhm in der Luft.

Dennoch, wir wissen ihn nicht zu nennen, wir raten . . .
Und Erinnerung geht zu ihm über,
die wir von rufbaren Stunden erbaten.

VI

Rose, you majesty—once, to the ancients, you were
just a calyx with the simplest of rims.
But for us, you are the full, the numberless flower,
the inexhaustible countenance.

In your wealth you seem to be wearing gown upon gown
upon a body of nothing but light;
yet each separate petal is at the same time the negation
of all clothing and the refusal of it.

Your fragrance has been calling its sweetest names
in our direction, for hundreds of years;
suddenly it hangs in the air like fame.

Even so, we have never known what to call it; we
        guess . . .
And memory is filled with it unawares
which we prayed for from hours that belong to us.

VII

Blumen, ihr schließlich den ordnenden Händen verwandte,
(Händen der Mädchen von einst und jetzt),
die auf dem Gartentisch oft von Kante zu Kante
lagen, ermattet und sanft verletzt,

wartend des Wassers, das sie noch einmal erhole ·
aus dem begonnenen Tod—, und nun
wieder erhobene zwischen die strömenden Pole
fühlender Finger, die wohlzutun

mehr noch vermögen, als ihr ahntet, ihr leichten,
wenn ihr euch wiederfandet im Krug,
langsam erkühlend und Warmes der Mädchen, wie Beichten,

von euch gebend, wie trübe ermüdende Sünden,
die das Gepflücktsein beging, als Bezug
wieder zu ihnen, die sich euch blühend verbünden.

VII

Flowers, you who are kin to the hands that arrange
(gentle girls' hands of present and past),
who often lay on the garden table, from edge
to edge, exhausted and slightly bruised,

waiting for the water once more to bring you back whole
from the death that had just begun—and now
lifted again between the fast-streaming poles
of sensitive fingers that are able to do

even more good than you guessed, as you lightly uncurled,
coming to yourselves again in the pitcher,
slowly cooling, and exhaling the warmth of girls

like long confessions, like dreary wearying sins
committed by being plucked, which once more
relate you to those who in blossoming are your cousins.

VIII

Wenige ihr, der einstigen Kindheit Gespielen
in den zerstreuten Gärten der Stadt:
wie wir uns fanden und uns zögernd gefielen
und, wie das Lamm mit dem redenden Blatt,

sprachen als Schweigende. Wenn wir uns einmal freuten,
keinem gehörte es. Wessen wars?
Und wie zergings unter allen den gehenden Leuten
und im Bangen des langen Jahrs.

Wagen umrollten uns fremd, vorübergezogen,
Häuser umstanden uns stark, aber unwahr,—und keines
kannte uns je. Was war wirklich im All?

Nichts. Nur die Bälle. Ihre herrlichen Bogen.
Auch nicht die Kinder . . . Aber manchmal trat eines,
ach ein vergehendes, unter den fallenden Ball.

(In memoriam Egon von Rilke)

VIII

You playmates of mine in the scattered parks of the city,
small friends from a childhood of long ago:
how we found and liked one another, hesitantly,
and, like the lamb with the talking scroll,

spoke with our silence. When we were filled with joy,
it belonged to no one: it was simply there.
And how it dissolved among all the adults who passed by
and in the fears of the endless year.

Wheels rolled past us, we stood and stared at the carriages;
houses surrounded us, solid but untrue—and none
of them ever knew us. *What* in that world was real?

Nothing. Only the balls. Their magnificent arches.
Not even the children . . . But sometimes one,
oh a vanishing one, stepped under the plummeting ball.

(In memoriam Egon von Rilke)

IX

Rühmt euch, ihr Richtenden, nicht der entbehrlichen Folter
und daß das Eisen nicht länger an Hälsen sperrt.
Keins ist gesteigert, kein Herz—, weil ein gewollter
Krampf der Milde euch zarter verzerrt.

Was es durch Zeiten bekam, das schenkt das Schafott
wieder zurück, wie Kinder ihr Spielzeug vom vorig
alten Geburtstag. Ins reine, ins hohe, ins thorig
offene Herz träte er anders, der Gott

wirklicher Milde. Er käme gewaltig und griffe
strahlender um sich, wie Göttliche sind.
Mehr als ein Wind für die großen gesicherten Schiffe.

Weniger nicht, als die heimliche leise Gewahrung,
die uns im Innern schweigend gewinnt
wie ein still spielendes Kind aus unendlicher Paarung.

IX

Don't boast, you judges, that you have dispensed with
      torture
and that convicts are no longer shackled by the neck or
      heel.
No heart is enhanced, not one is—because a tender
spasm of mercy twists your mouths into a smile.

What the scaffold received through the ages, it has given
      back
again, as children give back their battered old
birthday toys. Into the pure and lofty and gatelike
open heart he would differently enter, the god

of true mercy. Sudden, huge, he would stride through and
      grip
us dazzled with radiance all around.
More than a wind for the massive confident ships.

And not any less transforming than the deep intuition
that wins us over without a sound
like a quietly playing child of an infinite union.

X

Alles Erworbne bedroht die Maschine, solange
sie sich erdreistet, im Geist, statt im Gehorchen, zu sein.
Daß nicht der herrlichen Hand schöneres Zögern mehr prange,
zu dem entschlossenern Bau schneidet sie steifer den Stein.

Nirgends bleibt sie zurück, daß wir ihr ein Mal entrönnen
und sie in stiller Fabrik ölend sich selber gehört.
Sie ist das Leben,—sie meint es am besten zu können,
die mit dem gleichen Entschluß ordnet und schafft und
        zerstört.

Aber noch ist uns das Dasein verzaubert; an hundert
Stellen ist es noch Ursprung. Ein Spielen von reinen
Kräften, die keiner berührt, der nicht kniet und bewundert.

Worte gehen noch zart am Unsäglichen aus . . .
Und die Musik, immer neu, aus den bebendsten Steinen,
baut im unbrauchbaren Raum ihr vergöttlichtes Haus.

X

All we have gained the machine threatens, as long
as it dares to exist in the mind and not in obedience.
To dim the masterful hand's more glorious lingering,
for the determined structure it more rigidly cuts the
      stones.

Nowhere does it stay behind; we cannot escape it at last
as it rules, self-guided, self-oiled, from its silent factory.
It thinks it is life: thinks it does everything best,
though with equal determination it can create or destroy.

But still, existence for us is a miracle; in a hundred
places it is still the source. A playing of absolute
forces that no one can touch who has not knelt down in
      wonder.

Still there are words that can calmly approach the
      unsayable . . .
And from the most tremulous stones music, forever new,
builds in unusable space her deified temple.

XI

Manche, des Todes, entstand ruhig geordnete Regel,
weiterbezwingender Mensch, seit du im Jagen beharrst;
mehr doch als Falle und Netz, weiß ich dich, Streifen von
      Segel,
den man hinuntergehängt in den höhligen Karst.

Leise ließ man dich ein, als wärst du ein Zeichen,
Frieden zu feiern. Doch dann: rang dich am Rande der
      Knecht,
—und, aus den Höhlen, die Nacht warf eine Handvoll von
      bleichen
taumelnden Tauben ins Licht . . .
                              Aber auch das *ist im Recht.*

Fern von dem Schauenden sei jeglicher Hauch des
      Bedauerns,
nicht nur vom Jäger allein, der, was sich zeitig erweist,
wachsam und handelnd vollzieht.

Töten ist eine Gestalt unseres wandernden Trauerns . . .
Rein ist im heiteren Geist,
was an uns selber geschieht.

XI

Many calmly established rules of death have arisen,
ever-conquering man, since you acquired a taste
for hunting; yet more than all traps, I know you, sailcloths
       of linen
that used to be hung down into the caverns of Karst.

Gently they lowered you in as if you were a signal
to celebrate peace. But then: the boy began shaking your
       side,
—and suddenly, from the caves, the darkness would fling
       out a handful
of pale doves into the day . . .
                              But even that is all right.

Let every last twinge of pity be far from those who look
       on—
far not just from the conscience of the vigilant, steadfast
       hunter
who fulfills what time has allowed.

Killing too is a form of our ancient wandering affliction . . .
When the mind stays serene, whatever
happens to us is good.

XII

Wolle die Wandlung. O sei für die Flamme begeistert,
drin sich ein Ding dir entzieht, das mit Verwandlungen
         prunkt;
jener entwerfende Geist, welcher das Irdische meistert,
liebt in dem Schwung der Figur nichts wie den wendenden
         Punkt.

Was sich ins Bleiben verschließt, schon ists das Erstarrte;
wähnt es sich sicher im Schutz des unscheinbaren Grau's?
Warte, ein Härtestes warnt aus der Ferne das Harte.
Wehe—: abwesender Hammer holt aus!

Wer sich als Quelle ergießt, den erkennt die Erkennung;
und sie führt ihn entzückt durch das heiter Geschaffne,
das mit Anfang oft schließt und mit Ende beginnt.

Jeder glückliche Raum ist Kind oder Enkel von Trennung,
den sie staunend durchgehn. Und die verwandelte Daphne
will, seit sie lorbeern fühlt, daß du dich wandelst in Wind.

XII

Will transformation. Oh be inspired for the flame
in which a Thing disappears and bursts into something
       else;
the spirit of re-creation which masters this earthly form
loves most the pivoting point where you are no longer
       yourself.

What tightens into survival is already inert;
how safe is it really in its inconspicuous gray?
From far off a far greater hardness warns what is hard,
and the absent hammer is lifted high!

He who pours himself out like a stream is acknowledged
       at last by Knowledge;
and she leads him enchanted through the harmonious
       country
that finishes often with starting, and with ending begins.

Every fortunate space that the two of them pass through,
       astonished,
is a child or grandchild of parting. And the transfigured
       Daphne,
as she feels herself become laurel, wants you to change
       into wind.

XIII

Sei allem Abschied voran, als wäre er hinter
dir, wie der Winter, der eben geht.
Denn unter Wintern ist einer so endlos Winter,
daß, überwinternd, dein Herz überhaupt übersteht.

Sei immer tot in Eurydike—, singender steige,
preisender steige zurück in den reinen Bezug.
Hier, unter Schwindenden, sei, im Reiche der Neige,
sei ein klingendes Glas, das sich im Klang schon zerschlug.

Sei—und wisse zugleich des Nicht-Seins Bedingung,
den unendlichen Grund deiner innigen Schwingung,
daß du sie völlig vollziehst dieses einzige Mal.

Zu dem gebrauchten sowohl, wie zum dumpfen und stummen
Vorrat der vollen Natur, den unsäglichen Summen,
zähle dich jubelnd hinzu und vernichte die Zahl.

XlII

Be ahead of all parting, as though it already were
behind you, like the winter that has just gone by.
For among these winters there is one so endlessly winter
that only by wintering through it will your heart survive.

Be forever dead in Eurydice—more gladly arise
into the seamless life proclaimed in your song.
Here, in the realm of decline, among momentary days,
be the crystal cup that shattered even as it rang.

Be—and yet know the great void where all things begin,
the infinite source of your own most intense vibration,
so that, this once, you may give it your perfect assent.

To all that is used-up, and to all the muffled and dumb
creatures in the world's full reserve, the unsayable sums,
joyfully add your*self*, and cancel the count.

XIV

Siehe die Blumen, diese dem Irdischen treuen,
denen wir Schicksal vom Rande des Schicksals leihn,—
aber wer weiß es! Wenn sie ihr Welken bereuen,
ist es an uns, ihre Reue zu sein.

Alles will schweben. Da gehn wir umher wie Beschwerer,
legen auf alles uns selbst, vom Gewichte entzückt;
o was sind wir den Dingen für zehrende Lehrer,
weil ihnen ewige Kindheit glückt.

Nähme sie einer ins innige Schlafen und schliefe
tief mit den Dingen—: o wie käme er leicht,
anders zum anderen Tag, aus der gemeinsamen Tiefe.

Oder er bliebe vielleicht; und sie blühten und priesen
ihn, den Bekehrten, der nun den Ihrigen gleicht,
allen den stillen Geschwistern im Winde der Wiesen.

XIV

Look at the flowers, so faithful to what is earthly,
to whom we lend fate from the very border of fate.
And if they are sad about how they must wither and die,
perhaps it is our vocation to be their regret.

All Things want to fly. Only *we* are weighed down by
      desire,
caught in ourselves and enthralled with our heaviness.
Oh what consuming, negative teachers we are
for them, while eternal childhood fills them with grace.

If someone were to fall into intimate slumber, and slept
deeply with Things—: how easily he would come
to a different day, out of the mutual depth.

Or perhaps he would stay there; and they would blossom
      and praise
their newest convert, who now is like one of them,
all those silent companions in the wind of the meadows.

XV

O Brunnen-Mund, du gebender, du Mund,
der unerschöpflich Eines, Reines, spricht,—
du, vor des Wassers fließendem Gesicht,
marmorne Maske. Und im Hintergrund

der Aquädukte Herkunft. Weither an
Gräbern vorbei, vom Hang des Apennins
tragen sie dir dein Sagen zu, das dann
am schwarzen Altern deines Kinns

vorüberfällt in das Gefäß davor.
Dies ist das schlafend hingelegte Ohr,
das Marmorohr, in das du immer sprichst.

Ein Ohr der Erde. Nur mit sich allein
redet sie also. Schiebt ein Krug sich ein,
so scheint es ihr, daß du sie unterbrichst.

XV

O fountain-mouth, you generous, always-filled
mouth that speaks pure oneness, constantly—
you marble mask before the water's still
flowing face. And in the background, the

slow descent of aqueducts. From far
graves, and from the sloping Apennines,
they bring you all your syllables, which pour
down from your blackened, aging chin

into the basin lying underneath.
This is the close and sleeping ear, the ear
of marble, into which you always speak.

Earth's ear. To it alone she talks this way.
If you insert a jug, she feels you are
interrupting what she wants to say.

XVI

Immer wieder von uns aufgerissen,
ist der Gott die Stelle, welche heilt.
Wir sind Scharfe, denn wir wollen wissen,
aber er ist heiter und verteilt.

Selbst die reine, die geweihte Spende
nimmt er anders nicht in seine Welt,
als indem er sich dem freien Ende
unbewegt entgegenstellt.

Nur der Tote trinkt
aus der hier vons uns gehörten *Quelle*,
wenn der Gott ihm schweigend winkt, dem Toten.

Uns *wird nur das Lärmen angeboten.*
Und das Lamm erbittet seine Schelle
aus dem stilleren Instinkt.

XVI

Over and over by us torn in two,
the god is the hidden place that heals again.
We are sharp-edged, because we want to know,
but he is always scattered and serene.

Even the pure, the consecrated gift
he takes into his world no other way
than by positioning himself, unmoved,
to face the one end that is free.

Only the dead may drink
from the source that we just hear, the unseen pool,
when the god, mute, allows them with a gesture.

Here, to us, only the noise is offered.
And the lamb keeps begging for its bell
because of a more quiet instinct.

XVII

Wo, in welchen immer selig bewässerten Gärten, an welchen
Bäumen, aus welchen zärtlich entblätterten Blüten-Kelchen
reifen die fremdartigen Früchte der Tröstung? Diese
köstlichen, deren du eine vielleicht in der zertretenen Wiese

deiner Armut findest. Von einem zum anderen Male
wunderst du dich über die Größe der Frucht,
über ihr Heilsein, über die Sanftheit der Schale,
und daß sie der Leichtsinn des Vogels dir nicht vorwegnahm
         und nicht die Eifersucht

unten des Wurms. Giebt es denn Bäume, von Engeln
         beflogen,
und von verborgenen langsamen Gärtnern so seltsam gezogen,
daß sie uns tragen, ohne uns zu gehören?

Haben wir niemals vermocht, wir Schatten und Schemen,
durch unser voreilig reifes und wieder welkes Benehmen
jener gelassenen Sommer Gleichmut zu stören?

XVII

Where, inside what forever blissfully watered gardens,
      upon what trees,
out of what deep and tenderly unpetaled flower-cups,
do the exotic fruits of consolation hang ripening? Those
rare delicacies, of which you find one perhaps

in the trampled meadows of your poverty. Time and again
you have stood there marveling over the sheer size of the
      fruit,
over its wholeness, its smooth and unmottled skin,
and that the lightheaded bird or the jealous worm under
      the ground had not

snatched it away from your hands. *Are* there such trees,
      flown through
by angels and so strangely cared for by gardeners hidden
      and slow
that they bear their fruit to nourish us, without being
      ours?

Is it true we have never been able (we who are only
shadows and shades), through our ripening and wilting so
      early,
to disturb the enormous calm of those patient summers?

XVIII

Tänzerin: o du Verlegung
alles Vergehens in Gang: wie brachtest du's dar.
Und der Wirbel am Schluß, dieser Baum aus Bewegung,
nahm er nicht ganz in Besitz das erschwungene Jahr?

Blühte nicht, daß ihn dein Schwingen von vorhin
       umschwärme,
plötzlich sein Wipfel von Stille? Und über ihr,
war sie nicht Sonne, war sie nicht Sommer, die Wärme,
diese unzählige Wärme aus dir?

Aber er trug auch, er trug, dein Baum der Ekstase.
Sind sie nicht seine ruhigen Früchte: der Krug,
reifend gestreift, und die gereiftere Vase?

Und in den Bildern: ist nicht die Zeichnung geblieben,
die deiner Braue dunkler Zug
rasch an die Wandung der eigenen Wendung geschrieben?

XVIII

Dancing girl: transformation
of all transience into steps: how you offered it there.
And the arm-raised whirl at the end, that tree made of
      motion,
didn't it fully possess the pivoted year?

Didn't it, so that your previous swirling might swarm
in the midst of it, suddenly blossom with stillness? And
      above,
wasn't it sunshine, wasn't it summer, the warmth,
the pure, immeasurable warmth that you gave?

But it bore fruit also, it bore fruit, your tree of bliss.
Aren't they here in their tranquil season: the jug,
whirling to ripeness, and the even more ripened vase?

And in the pictures: can't we still see the drawing
which your eyebrow's dark evanescent stroke
quickly inscribed on the surface of its own turning?

XIX

Irgendwo wohnt das Gold in der verwöhnenden Bank
und mit Tausenden tut es vertraulich. Doch jener
Blinde, der Bettler, ist selbst dem kupfernen Zehner
wie ein verlorener Ort, wie das staubige Eck unterm Schrank.

In den Geschäften entlang ist das Geld wie zuhause
und verkleidet sich scheinbar in Seide, Nelken und Pelz.
Er, der Schweigende, steht in der Atempause
alles des wach oder schlafend atmenden Gelds.

O wie mag sie sich schließen bei Nacht, diese immer offene
        Hand.
Morgen holt sie das Schicksal wieder, und täglich
hält es sie hin: hell, elend, unendlich zerstörbar.

Daß doch einer, ein Schauender, endlich ihren langen Bestand
staunend begriffe und rühmte. Nur dem Aufsingenden
        säglich.
Nur dem Göttlichen hörbar.

XIX

Somewhere gold lives, luxurious, inside the pampering
      bank,
on intimate terms with thousands. Meanwhile, the
      wretched
blindman begging here seems, even to a penny, just like
some always-forgotten corner or the dustpile beneath a
      bed.

In all the most elegant shops money is at ease
and steps out in shiny costumes of furs, carnations, and
      silks.
He, the silent one, stands in the narrow breath-pause
made by money breathing as it slumbers or wakes.

Oh how can it close at night, that hand which is always
      open?
Tomorrow and each day Fate will arrive and hold it out:
      clear,
squalid, at any moment likely to be destroyed.

If only someone who could *see*, astonished at its long
      duration,
would understand it and praise it. Sayable only to the
      singer.
Audible only to the god.

XX

Zwischen den Sternen, wie weit; und doch, um wievieles noch
      weiter,
was man am Hiesigen lernt.
Einer, zum Beispiel, ein Kind . . . und ein Nächster, ein
      Zweiter—,
o wie unfaßlich entfernt.

Schicksal, es mißt uns vielleicht mit des Seienden Spanne,
daß es uns fremd erscheint;
denk, wieviel Spannen allein vom Mädchen zum Manne,
wenn es ihn meidet und meint.

Alles ist weit—, und nirgends schließt sich der Kreis.
Sieh in der Schüssel, auf heiter bereitetem Tische,
seltsam der Fische Gesicht.

Fische sind stumm . . . , meinte man einmal. Wer weiß?
Aber ist nicht am Ende ein Ort, wo man das, was der Fische
Sprache wäre, ohne sie spricht?

XX

In between stars, what distances; and yet, how much
        vaster the distance
that we learn from what is right *here*.
Someone, for example a child . . . and beside him, his
        brother or sister—
oh how incomprehensibly far.

Fate measures us perhaps according to what is real,
so it seems to us not our own;
think of how vast a distance there is from the girl
to the loved and avoided man.

All things are far—and nowhere does the circle close.
Look at the fish, served up on the gaily set table:
how peculiar its face on the dish.

All fish are mute . . . , one used to think. But who knows?
Isn't there at last a place where, *without* them, we would
        be able
to speak in the language of fish?

XXI

Singe die Gärten, mein Herz, die du nicht kennst; wie in Glas
eingegossene Gärten, klar, unerreichbar.
Wasser und Rosen von Ispahan oder Schiras,
singe sie selig, preise sie, keinem vergleichbar.

Zeige, mein Herz, daß du sie niemals entbehrst.
Daß sie dich meinen, ihre reifenden Feigen.
Daß du mit ihren, zwischen den blühenden Zweigen
wie zum Gesicht gesteigerten Lüften verkehrst.

Meide den Irrtum, daß es Entbehrungen gebe
für den geschehnen Entschluß, diesen: zu sein!
Seidener Faden, kamst du hinein ins Gewebe.

Welchem der Bilder du auch im Innern geeint bist
(sei es selbst ein Moment aus dem Leben der Pein),
fühl, daß der ganze, der rühmliche Teppich gemeint ist.

XXl

Sing of the gardens, my heart, that you never saw; as if
     glass
domes had been placed upon them, unreached forever.
Fountains and roses of Ispahan or Shiraz—
sing of their happiness, praise them: unlike all others.

Show that you always feel them, forever close.
That when their figs ripen, it is you they are ripening for.
That you know every breeze which, among the blossoms
     they bear,
is intensified till it almost becomes a face.

Avoid the illusion that there can be any lack
for someone who wishes, then fully decides: to be!
Silken thread, you were woven into the fabric.

Whatever the design with which you are inwardly joined
(even for only one moment amid years of grief),
feel that the whole, the marvelous carpet is meant.

XXII

O trotz Schicksal: die herrlichen Überflüsse
unseres Daseins, in Parken übergeschäumt,—
oder als steinerne Männer neben die Schlüsse
hoher Portale, unter Balkone gebäumt!

O die eherne Glocke, die ihre Keule
täglich wider den stumpfen Alltag hebt.
Oder die eine, in Karnak, die Säule, die Säule,
die fast ewige Tempel überlebt.

Heute stürzen die Überschüsse, dieselben,
nur noch als Eile vorbei, aus dem waagrechten gelben
Tag in die blendend mit Licht übertriebene Nacht.

Aber das Rasen zergeht und läßt keine Spuren.
Kurven des Flugs durch die Luft und die, die sie fuhren,
keine vielleicht ist umsonst. Doch nur wie gedacht.

XXII

Oh in spite of fate: the glorious overflowings
of our existence, spouted upward in parks—
or as stone-carved men who bear upon shoulders and
          backs
the weight overhead, braced on the sheer edge of
          buildings.

Oh the bronze bell that, day after day, can lift
its club to shatter our dull quotidian hum.
Or the *only* presence, in Karnak, the column, the column
in which temples that were almost eternal have been
          outlived.

For us these abundances plunge past, no longer central
but only appearing as haste, out of the horizontal
yellow day and into the overwhelmed, dazzled night.

But this frenzy too will subside, leaving no traces.
Arcs of airplanes and those who drove them through
          space,
none perhaps is in vain. Yet only as thought.

XXIII

Rufe mich zu jener deiner Stunden,
die dir unaufhörlich widersteht:
flehend nah wie das Gesicht von Hunden,
aber immer wieder weggedreht,

wenn du meinst, sie endlich zu erfassen.
So Entzognes ist am meisten dein.
Wir sind frei. Wir wurden dort entlassen,
wo wir meinten, erst begrüßt zu sein.

Bang verlangen wir nach einem Halte,
wir zu Jungen manchmal für das Alte
und zu alt für das, was niemals war.

Wir, gerecht nur, wo wir dennoch preisen,
weil wir, ach, der Ast sind und das Eisen
und das Süße reifender Gefahr.

XXIII

Call me to the one among your moments
that stands against you, ineluctably:
intimate as a dog's imploring glance
but, again, forever, turned away

when you think you've captured it at last.
What seems so far from you is most your own.
We are already free, and were dismissed
where we thought we soon would be at home.

Anxious, we keep longing for a foothold—
we, at times too young for what is old
and too old for what has never been;

doing justice only where we praise,
because we are the branch, the iron blade,
and sweet danger, ripening from within.

XXIV

O diese Lust, immer neu, aus gelockertem Lehm!
Niemand beinah hat den frühesten Wagern geholfen.
Städte entstanden trotzdem an beseligten Golfen,
Wasser und Öl füllten die Krüge trotzdem.

Götter, wir planen sie erst in erkühnten Entwürfen,
die uns das mürrische Schicksal wieder zerstört.
Aber sie sind die Unsterblichen. Sehet, wir dürfen
jenen erhorchen, der uns am Ende erhört.

Wir, ein Geschlecht durch Jahrtausende: Mütter und Väter,
immer erfüllter von dem künftigen Kind,
daß es uns einst, übersteigend, erschüttere, später.

Wir, wir unendlich Gewagten, was haben wir Zeit!
Und nur der schweigsame Tod, der weiß, was wir sind
und was er immer gewinnt, wenn er uns leiht.

XXIV

Oh the delight, ever new, out of loosened soil!
The ones who first dared were almost without any help.
Nonetheless, at fortunate harbors, cities sprang up,
and pitchers were nonetheless filled with water and oil.

Gods: we project them first in the boldest of sketches,
which sullen Fate keeps crumpling and tossing away.
But for all that, the gods are immortal. Surely we may
hear out the one who, in the end, will hear *us*.

We, one generation through thousands of lifetimes:
      women
and men, who are more and more filled with the child we
      will bear,
so that through it we may be shattered and overtaken.

We, the endlessly dared—how far we have come!
And only taciturn Death can know what we are
and how he must always profit when he lends us time.

XXV

Schon, horch, hörst du der ersten Harken
Arbeit; wieder den menschlichen Takt
in der verhaltenen Stille der starken
Vorfrühlingserde. Unabgeschmackt

scheint dir das Kommende. Jenes so oft
dir schon Gekommene scheint dir zu kommen
wieder wie Neues. Immer erhofft,
nahmst du es niemals. Es hat dich genommen.

Selbst die Blätter durchwinterter Eichen
scheinen im Abend ein künftiges Braun.
Manchmal geben sich Lüfte ein Zeichen.

Schwarz sind die Sträucher. Doch Haufen von Dünger
lagern als satteres Schwarz in den Aun.
Jede Stunde, die hingeht, wird jünger.

XXV

Already (listen!) you can hear the first
harrows; once more the rhythm of men
through the held-back silence of the resolute earth
in early spring. What has so often

come to you is coming once more,
vivid as if for the first time. Now,
slowly, you await what you always hoped for
but never took. It always took *you*.

Even the leaves of wintered-through oaks
seem in the twilight a future brown.
Breezes signal, then signal back.

Black are the bushes. Yet heaps of dung
lie more intensely black on the ground.
Every hour that goes by grows younger.

XXVI

Wie ergreift uns der Vogelschrei . . .
Irgend ein einmal erschaffenes Schreien.
Aber die Kinder schon, spielend im Freien,
schreien an wirklichen Schreien vorbei.

Schreien den Zufall. In Zwischenräume
dieses, des Weltraums, (in welchen der heile
Vogelschrei eingeht, wie Menschen in Träume—)
treiben sie ihre, des Kreischens, Keile.

Wehe, wo sind wir? Immer noch freier,
wie die losgerissenen Drachen
jagen wir halbhoch, mit Rändern von Lachen,

windig zerfetzten.—Ordne die Schreier,
singender Gott! daß sie rauschend erwachen,
tragend als Strömung das Haupt und die Leier.

XXVI

How deeply the cry of a bird can move us . . .
Any cry that is cried out whole.
But children, playing in their open space—
already their cries have become unreal.

They cry out chance. And into the silent
seamless world, into which birds' cries
fully (as men into dream-space) blend,
they hammer the hard-edged wedge of their noise.

Alas, where are we? Freer and freer,
like colored kites torn loose from their strings,
we toss half-high-up, framed by cold laughter,

slashed by the wind.—Oh compose the criers,
harmonious god! let them wake resounding,
let their clear stream carry the head and the lyre.

XXVII

Giebt es wirklich die Zeit, die zerstörende?
Wann, auf dem ruhenden Berg, zerbricht sie die Burg?
Dieses Herz, das unendlich den Göttern gehörende,
wann vergewaltigts der Demiurg?

Sind wir wirklich so ängstlich Zerbrechliche,
wie das Schicksal uns wahr machen will?
Ist die Kindheit, die tiefe, versprechliche,
in den Wurzeln—später—still?

Ach, das Gespenst des Vergänglichen,
durch den arglos Empfänglichen
geht es, als wär es ein Rauch.

Als die, die wir sind, als die Treibenden,
gelten wir doch bei bleibenden
Kräften als göttlicher Brauch.

XXVII

Does it really exist, Time, the Destroyer?
When will it crush the fortress on the peaceful height?
This heart, which belongs to the infinite gods forever,
when will the Demiurge violate *it*?

Are we really as fate keeps trying to convince us,
weak and brittle in an alien world?
And childhood, with all its divining voices,
is it later, down to its first root, stilled?

Ah, the ghost of the transient
moves through the open, innocent
heart like a summer cloud.

As who we are, desperate, driving,
we still matter among the abiding
powers as a use of the gods.

XXVIII

O komm und geh. Du, fast noch Kind, ergänze
für einen Augenblick die Tanzfigur
zum reinen Sternbild einer jener Tänze,
darin wir die dumpf ordnende Natur

vergänglich übertreffen. Denn sie regte
sich völlig hörend nur, da Orpheus sang.
Du warst noch die von damals her Bewegte
und leicht befremdet, wenn ein Baum sich lang

besann, mit dir nach dem Gehör zu gehn.
Du wußtest noch die Stelle, wo die Leier
sich tönend hob—; die unerhörte Mitte.

Für sie versuchtest du die schönen Schritte
und hofftest, einmal zu der heilen Feier
des Freundes Gang und Antlitz hinzudrehn.

XXVIII

Oh come and go. You, almost still a child—
for just a moment fill out the dance-figure
into the constellation of those bold
dances in which dull, obsessive Nature

is fleetingly surpassed. For she was stirred
to total hearing just when Orpheus sang.
You were still moved by those primeval words
and a bit surprised if any tree took long

to step with you into the listening ear.
You knew the place where once the lyre arose
resounding: the unheard, unheard-of center.

For *its* sake you tried out your lovely motion
and hoped that you would one day turn your friend's
body toward the perfect celebration.

XXIX

Stiller Freund der vielen Fernen, fühle,
wie dein Atem noch den Raum vermehrt.
Im Gebälk der finstern Glockenstühle
laß dich läuten. Das, was an dir zehrt,

wird ein Starkes über dieser Nahrung.
Geh in der Verwandlung aus und ein.
Was ist deine leidendste Erfahrung?
Ist dir Trinken bitter, werde Wein.

Sei in dieser Nacht aus Übermaß
Zauberkraft am Kreuzweg deiner Sinne,
ihrer seltsamen Begegnung Sinn.

Und wenn dich das Irdische vergaß,
zu der stillen Erde sag: Ich rinne.
Zu dem raschen Wasser sprich: Ich bin.

XXIX

Silent friend of many distances, feel
how your breath enlarges all of space.
Let your presence ring out like a bell
into the night. What feeds upon your face

grows mighty from the nourishment thus offered.
Move through transformation, out and in.
What is the deepest loss that you have suffered?
If drinking is bitter, change yourself to wine.

In this immeasurable darkness, be the power
that rounds your senses in their magic ring,
the sense of their mysterious encounter.

And if the earthly no longer knows your name,
whisper to the silent earth: I'm flowing.
To the flashing water say: I am.

APPENDIX

(1)

Rühmen, das ists! Ein zum Rühmen Bestellter,
ging er hervor wie das Erz aus des Steins
Schweigen. Sein Herz, o vergängliche Kelter
eines den Menschen unendlichen Weins!

Euch kanns beirren, wenn man in Grüften
Könige aufdeckt, verfault und verwürmt, —
ihm hat der Hinfall der Häupter und Hüften
zwar mit zehrendem Weh bestürmt,

aber der Zweifel war ihm verächtlich.
Er zerrang den Gestank und pries
Tägiges täglich und Nächtiges nächtlich,

denn wer erkennt die verwandelten Gnaden?
Knieend aus dem Markte der Maden
hob er das heile Goldene Vließ.

(1)

Praising is what matters! He was summoned for that,
and came to us like the ore from a stone's
silence. His mortal heart presses out
a deathless, inexhaustible wine!

Don't be confused if kings are discovered
rotting in their sepulchers, gnawed by the worm—
for a while the decay of body and head
assailed him too with intense alarm;

he, however, despising all doubt,
throttled the stench and with praise affirmed
the daily by day and the nightly at night,

for who knows what is transformed by the graces?
Kneeling from the maggots' marketplace,
he lifted the Golden Fleece, unharmed.

(11)

O das Neue, Freunde, ist nicht dies,
daß Maschinen uns die Hand verdrängen.
Laßt euch nicht beirrn von Übergängen,
bald wird schweigen, wer das ›Neue‹ pries.

Denn das Ganze ist unendlich neuer,
als ein Kabel und ein hohes Haus.
Seht, die Sterne sind ein altes Feuer,
und die neuern Feuer löschen aus.

Glaubt nicht, daß die längsten Transmissionen
schon des Künftigen Räder drehn.
Denn Aeonen reden mit Aeonen.

Mehr, als wir erfuhren, ist geschehn.
Und die Zukunft faßt das Allerfernste
rein in eins mit unserm innern Ernste.

(ll)

The New, my friends, is not a matter of
letting machines force out our handiwork.
Don't be confused by change; soon those who have
praised the "New" will realize their mistake.

For look, the Whole is infinitely newer
than a cable or a high apartment house.
The stars keep blazing with an ancient fire,
and all more recent fires will fade out.

Not even the longest, strongest of transmissions
can turn the wheels of what will be.
Across the moment, aeons speak with aeons.

More than we experienced has gone by.
And the future holds the most remote event
in union with what we most deeply want.

(III)

Brau uns den Zauber, in dem die Grenzen sich lösen,
immer zum Feuer gebeugter Geist!
Diese, vor allem, heimliche Grenze des Bösen,
die auch den Ruhenden, der sich nicht rührte, umkreist.

Löse mit einigen Tropfen das Engende jener
Grenze der Zeiten, die uns belügt;
denn wie tief ist in uns noch der Tag der Athener
und der ägyptische Gott oder Vogel gefügt.

Ruhe nicht eher, bis auch der Rand der Geschlechter,
der sich sinnlos verringenden, schmolz.
Öffne die Kindheit und die Schooße gerechter

gebender Mütter, daß sie, Beschämer der Leere,
unbeirrt durch das hindernde Holz
künftige Ströme gebären, Vermehrer der Meere.

(III)

Brew us the magic in which all limits dissolve,
spirit forever bent to the fire!
That fathomless limit of evil, first, which revolves
also around those who are resting and do not stir.

Dissolve with a few drops whatever excludes in the limit
of the ages, which makes our past wisdom a fraud;
for how deeply we have absorbed the Athenian sunlight
and the mystery of the Egyptian falcon or god.

Don't rest until the boundary that keeps the sexes
in meaningless conflict has disappeared.
Open up childhood and the wombs of more truly
       expectant

generous mothers so that, shaming all that is empty,
and not confused by the hindering wood,
they may give birth to future rivers, augmenting the sea.

(IV)

Mehr nicht sollst du wissen als die Stele
und im reinen Stein das milde Bild:
beinah heiter, nur so leicht als fehle
ihr die Mühe, die auf Erden gilt.

Mehr nicht sollst du fühlen als die reine
Richtung im unendlichen Entzug—
ach, vielleicht das Kaltsein jener Steine,
die sie manchmal abends trug.

Aber sonst sei dir die Tröstung teuer,
die du im Gewohntesten erkennst.
Wind ist Trost, und Tröstung ist das Feuer.

Hier- und Dortsein, dich ergreife beides
seltsam ohne Unterschied. Du trennst
sonst das Weißsein von dem Weiß des Kleides.

(IV)

Seek no more than what the stela knows,
and the mild image sculpted in the stone:
almost cheerfully, with a lightness, as
though they were exempt from earthly pain.

Experience no further than the pure
direction in the world's withdrawing stream—
ah, perhaps the icy jewels she wore
in that dimly lighted room.

Be all the more consoled by what you see in
the elements that are most truly yours.
Wind consoles, and fire is consolation.

Here and There: you must be gripped by both,
strangely without a difference. Otherwise
you drain the whiteness from the whitest cloth.

(V)

Denk: Sie hätten vielleicht aneinander erfahren,
welches die teilbaren Wunder sind—.
Doch da er sich langsam verrang an den alternden Jahren,
war sie die Künftige erst, ein kommendes Kind.

Sie, vielleicht—, sie, die da ging und mit Freundinnen spielte,
hat er im knabigen schon, im Erahnen, ersehnt,
wissend das schließende Herz, das ihn völlig enthielte,
und nun trennt sie ein Nichts, ein verfünftes Jahrzehnt.

Oh du ratloser Gott, du betrogener Hymen,
wie du die Fackel nach abwärts kehrst,
weil sie ihm Asche warf an die grauende Schläfe.

Soll er klagend vergehn und die Beginnende rühmen?
Oder sein stillster Verzicht, wird er sie erst
machen zu jener Gestalt, die ihn ganz überträfe?

(V)

Imagine: they might have experienced through each other
which of our miracles can be shared—.
But while he gradually wrestled with growing older,
she was as yet unborn, a still-future child.

She, perhaps—still playing with her friends, it was *she*
whom he had foreseen with boyish longing and love,
knowing the heart that would one day hold him
        completely;
and now a mere nothing parts them: a decade times five.

Oh you bewildered god, you defrauded Hymen,
how sadly you extinguish the wedding-torch now
because it flung ashes onto that graying head.

Must he die in laments, and praise the beginning woman?
Or through his most silent yielding will he make her into
that unmoving form by which he is wholly exceeded?

(VI)

Aber, ihr Freunde, zum Fest, laßt uns gedenken der Feste,
wenn uns ein eigenes nicht, mitten im Umzug, gelingt.
Seht, sie meinen auch uns, alle der Villa d'Este
spielende Brunnen, wenn auch nicht mehr ein jeglicher
                    springt.

Wir sind die Erben, trotzdem, dieser gesungenen Gärten;
Freunde, o faßt sie im Ernst, diese besitzende Pflicht.
Was uns als Letzten vielleicht glückliche Götter gewährten,
hat keinen ehrlichen Platz im zerstreuten Verzicht.

Keiner der Götter vergeh. Wir brauchen sie alle und jeden,
jedes gelte uns noch, jedes gestaltete Bild.
Laßt euch, was ruhig geruht, nicht in den Herzen zerreden.

Sind wir auch anders, als die, denen noch Feste gelangen,
dieser leistende Strahl, der uns als Stärke entquillt,
ist über große, zu uns, Aquädukte gegangen.

(VI)

When everything we create is far in spirit from the festive,
in the midst of our turbulent days let us think of what
      festivals *were*.
Look, they still play for us also, all of the Villa d'Este's
glittering fountains, though some are no longer towering
      there.

Still, we are heirs to those gardens that poets once praised
      in their songs;
let us grasp our most urgent duty: to make them fully our
      own.
We perhaps are the last to be given such god-favored,
      fortunate Things,
their final chance to find an enduring home.

Let not one god pass away. We all need each of them now,
let each be valid for us, each image formed in the depths.
Don't speak with the slightest disdain of whatever the
      heart can know.

Though we are no longer the ones for whom great
      festivals thrived,
this accomplishing fountain-jet that surges to us as
      strength
has traveled through aqueducts—in order, for our sake, to
      arrive.

(VII)

Welche Stille um einen Gott! Wie hörst du in ihr
jeden Wechsel im Auffall des Brunnenstrahls
am weilenden Wasser des Marmorovals.
Und am Lorbeer vorüber ein Fühlen: drei oder vier

Blätter, die ein Falter gestreift hat. An dir
taumelt er hin, im tragenden Atem des Tals.
Und du gedenkst eines anderen Mals,
da sie dir schon so vollkommen schien, hier,

diese Stille um einen Gott. Ward sie nicht mehr?
Nimmt sie nicht zu? Nimmt sie nicht überhand?
Drängt sie nicht fast wie ein Widerstand

an dein tönendes Herz? Irgendwo bricht sich sein Schlag
an einer lautlosen Pause im Tag . . .
Dort ist Er.

(VII)

What silence around a god! How, inside it, you hear
every change in the sparkling fountain-spray
on the marble pool, as it leaps up and falls back entirely.
And over the laurel a feeling: three, perhaps four

leaves that a butterfly touched. With a whir
it goes tumbling past, on the buoyant breath of the valley.
And now you remember another day
when you felt it, already so perfect, here,

the silence around a god. But was it like this?
Isn't it spreading? Isn't it immense?
Isn't it pressing almost like a resistance

upon your resounding heart? Somewhere its beat is
      broken
on a soundless lull in the afternoon . . .
There, He is.

(VIII)

Wir hören seit lange die Brunnen mit.
Sie klingen uns beinah wie Zeit.
Aber sie halten viel eher Schritt
mit der wandelnden Ewigkeit.

Das Wasser ist fremd und das Wasser ist dein,
von hier und doch nicht von hier.
Eine Weile bist du der Brunnenstein,
und es spiegelt die Dinge in dir.

Wie ist das alles entfernt und verwandt
und lange enträtselt und unerkannt,
sinnlos und wieder voll Sinn.

Dein ist, zu lieben, was du nicht weißt.
Es nimmt dein geschenktes Gefühl und reißt
es mit sich hinüber. Wohin?

(VlIl)

We have overheard fountains all our days.
They sound to us almost like time.
But much more closely do they keep pace
with eternity's subtle rhythm.

The water is strange and the water is yours,
from here and from far below.
You are the fountain-stone, unawares,
and all Things are mirrored in you.

How distant this is, yet deeply akin,
long unriddled and never known,
senseless, then perfectly clear.

Your task is to love what you don't understand.
It grips your most secret emotion, and
rushes away with it. Where?

(IX)

Wann war ein Mensch je so wach
wie der Morgen von heut?
Nicht nur Blume und Bach,
auch das Dach ist erfreut.

Selbst sein alternder Rand,
von den Himmeln erhellt,—
wird fühlend: ist Land,
ist Antwort, ist Welt.

Alles atmet und dankt.
O ihr Nöte der Nacht,
wie ihr spurlos versankt.

Aus Scharen von Licht
war ihr Dunkel gemacht,
das sich rein widerspricht.

(IX)

When was a *man* as awake
as this morning is?
Not just flower and brook:
the roof too rejoices.

Even its weathered rim,
lit by the sky—
finds it can feel: is home,
is answer, is day.

Everything breathes in accord.
How tracelessly you have gone
away, you cares of the night.

Its darkness was formed,
in pure contradiction,
from legions of light.

(I)

So wie angehaltner Atem steht
steht die Nymphe in dem vollen Baume

(II)

Sieh hinauf. Heut ist der Nachtraum heiter.

(III)

Hoher Gott der fernen Vorgesänge
überall erfahr ich dich zutiefst
in der freien Ordnung mancher Hänge
stehn die Sträucher noch wie du sie riefst

(IV)

Spiegel, du Doppelgänger des Raums! O Spiegel, in dich fort
stürzt die Hälfte der Lächeln / vielleicht die süßesten; denn wie
oft dem Meister der Strich, der probende, auf dem
vorläufigen Blatt blumiger aufschwingt, als später
auf dem bereiteten Grund der geführtere Umriß:
So, oh, lächelst du hin, Unsägliche, deiner
Morgen Herkunft und Freiheit in die immer
nehmenden Spiegel

FRAGMENTS

(I)

Like held-in breath, serene and motionless
stands the nymph inside the ripening tree

(II)

Look up. How calm the heavens are tonight.

(III)

Lofty god of distant harmonies
I sense you everywhere deep in every Thing
upon the gently patterned slope the trees
stand silent as when first they heard you sing

(IV)

Mirror, you doppelgänger of space! O mirror, into you go
plunging the halves of smiles / perhaps the sweetest; for
      how
often the master's preliminary brushstroke, upon the
provisional page more fruitfully leaps up than, later,
the more controlled outline does on the ready
      background:
So do you, O unsayable presence, smile forth
your morning's descent and freedom into the ever-
accepting mirrors

(V)

Immer, o Nymphe, seit je / hab ich dich staunend bewundert
ob du auch nie aus dem Baum mir dem verschlossenen tratst—.
Ich bin die Zeit die vergeht—, du bist ein junges Jahrhundert,
alles ist immer noch neu, was du von Göttern erbatst.

Dein ist die Wiese, sie schwankt noch jetzt von dem Sprunge,
jenem mit dem du zuletzt in die Ulme verschwandst.
Einst in der christlichen Früh. Und ist nicht, du junge,
Dir unser erstes Gefühl in den Frühling gepflanzt.

Eh uns ein Mädchen noch rührt, bist du die gemeinte

(VI)

. . . . Braun's

. . . . an den sonoren
trockenen Boden des Walds
                    trommelt das Flüchten des Fauns

(VII)

Dies ist das schweigende Steigen der Phallen

(V)

Forever, O nymph, how long / I have marveled at you,
          amazed,
though you never stepped into my sight from out of the
          closed-in tree—.
I am the time that is passing—you are the youngest age,
all that you asked from the gods has remained here,
          forever new.

Yours is the meadow, even now it sways from the leap
with which you finally vanished into the elm.
Once, in the christian dawn. And our earliest hope:
for *your* sake isn't it planted into the springtime?

Before we are moved by a girl, it is you that we think of

(VI)

. . . . of the brown

. . . . on the sonorous
dried-up earth of the forest
                    drums the flight of the faun

(VII)

This is the silent rising of the phalli

(VIII)

Von meiner Antwort weiß ich noch nicht
wann ich sie sagen werde.
Aber, horch eine Harke, die schon schafft.
Oben allein im Weinberg spricht
schon ein Mann mit der Erde.

(IX)

Hast du des Epheus wechselnde Blättergestalten

(X)

Wahre dich besser
        wahre dich Wandrer
mit dem selber auch gehenden Weg

(XI)

Laß uns Legenden der Liebe hören.
Zeig uns ihr kühnes köstliches Leid.
Wo sie im Recht war, war alles Beschwören,
hier ist das meiste verleugneter Eid.

(VIII)

About my answer: I still don't know
when I will bring it forth.
But listen, a harrow that already creates.
Up there in the vineyard someone, alone,
already speaks with the earth.

(IX)

Have you [?ever observed] the changing leaf-forms of the
        ivy

(X)

Protect yourself better
                protect yourself wanderer
with the road that is walking too

(XI)

Gather us now to hear love's legends.
Tell us of its daring, exquisite throes.
Where it was right, all things could be summoned;
here there are mostly abandoned vows.

NOTES

The German text and the dating is that of the standard edition, *Sämtliche Werke* (SW), edited by Ernst Zinn, Frankfurt am Main: Insel Verlag, 1955–1966. Letters excerpted in these notes come from the following sources:

Briefe aus Muzot, 1921–1926, Leipzig: Insel Verlag, 1937.

Briefe, Wiesbaden: Insel Verlag, 1950.

Rainer Maria Rilke und Marie von Thurn und Taxis: Briefwechsel, Zürich / Wiesbaden: Niehans & Rokitansky Verlag und Insel Verlag, 1951.

Rainer Maria Rilke / Lou Andreas-Salomé: Briefwechsel, Wiesbaden: Insel Verlag, 1954.

Rainer Maria Rilke / Katharina Kippenberg: Briefwechsel, Wiesbaden: Insel Verlag, 1954.

Briefe an Nanny Wunderly-Volkart, Frankfurt am Main: Insel Verlag, 1977.

INTRODUCTION

page 7
"as though, from far off . . .": "Self-Portrait, 1906," *The Selected Poetry of Rainer Maria Rilke*, New York: Random House, 1982, p. 41.

page 7
famous scene: See *The Selected Poetry*, p. 315.

page 8
"hurricane in the spirit": To Princess Marie von Thurn und Taxis-Hohenlohe, February 11, 1922.

page 8
"howling . . .": To Nanny Wunderly-Volkart, February 15, 1922.

page 8
by February 23: The chronology is as follows: Between the 2nd and 5th: Sonnets I,1–6, 8–20, 22, 24–26, [I–II], and fragments i–iii. 7th: the Seventh Elegy. 7th–8th: the Eighth Elegy. 9th: almost all

of the Ninth Elegy, Sonnet I,21, almost all of the original Fifth Elegy, one short poem, and the end of the Sixth Elegy. 11th: most of the Tenth Elegy. 12th–15th: "The Young Workman's Letter," Sonnet I,23, one short poem, fragment iv, and the new Fifth Elegy. 15th–17th: Sonnets II,5–6, 2–4, 7–15, [III–VII], fragments v–vi, and one short poem. 17th–23rd: Sonnets II,16–29, I,7, II,1, [VIII–IX], fragments vii–xii (one of which I have omitted), and two short poems.

page 8
sixty-four Sonnets: These vary in quality, of course. Six of the Sonnets, for me, rank very high among the supreme poems of the world: II,29, II,13, I,3, I,2, II,1, and II,12. The other great Sonnets, in my opinion, are I,1, 5, 6, 9–13, 16, 19–22, 25, II,2–6, 8, 14–16, 23–24, 28, [III–IV], and [VII–VIII]. Of the rest, the weaker poems are I,18, 23–24, II, 7, 10, 19, 21, [I–II], and [VI].

page 8
"incandescence of the intelligence": Wallace Stevens. Even he, a cool customer among the great poets, mentions this fulfillment in the most ardent terms, which can be applied to no poems better than to the late Elegies and the Sonnets: "If, then, when we speak of liberation, we mean an exodus; if when we speak of justification, we mean a kind of justice of which we had not known and on which we had not counted; if when we experience a sense of purification, we can think of the establishing of a self, it is certain that the experience of the poet is of no less a degree than the experience of the mystic and we may be certain that in the case of poets, the peers of saints, these experiences are of no less a degree than the experiences of the saints themselves." (*The Necessary Angel,* New York: Knopf, 1951, pp. 60, 50f.)

page 9
without desire: "Song, as you teach it, is not desire, / not wooing for anything that can be finally attained. . . ." (I,3); "Nowhere without Not: the Pure, / Un-overwatched, which one breathes and / endlessly *knows* and does not desire." (Eighth Elegy)

page 9
Meister Eckhart: Meister Eckhart: A Modern Translation, by Raymond Bernard Blakney, New York: Harper & Row, 1941, p. 95.

page 9
"The more poetic, the more real": "Die Poesie ist das echt absolut Reelle. Dies ist der Kern meiner Philosophie. Je poetischer, je

wahrer." *Neue Fragmente,* in *Briefe und Werke,* vol. 3, Berlin: Verlag Lambert Schneider, 1943, p. 118.

page 9
four times afterward: In I,25, II,13, 18, 28.

page 9
"When man is fast asleep . . .": Chhandogya Upanishad, *The Ten Principal Upanishads,* translated by W. B. Yeats and Shri Purohit Swami, New York: Macmillan, 1937, p. 115. Ramana Maharshi, the wisest of twentieth-century teachers, explains: "When passing from sleep to waking the 'I' thought must start; the mind comes into play; thoughts arise; and then the functions of the body come into operation; all these together make us say that we are awake. The absence of all this evolution is the characteristic of dreamless sleep and therefore it is nearer to pure consciousness than the waking state." The analogy isn't exact, however. "The state of the sage is neither sleep nor waking. It is the state of perfect awareness and of perfect stillness combined. It lies between sleep and waking; it is also the interval between two successive thoughts. . . . If you go to the root of thoughts, you reach the stillness of sleep. But you reach it in the full vigor of search, that is, with perfect awareness. It is not dullness but bliss. It is not transitory but eternal." (*Talks with Sri Ramana Maharshi,* Sixth Edition, Tiruvannamalai: Sri Ramanasramam, 1978, pp. 563f.)

page 10
the name of God: Exodus 3:14.

page 10
connection with Novalis: For the uncanny stories, see *The Way of the White Clouds: A Buddhist Pilgrim in Tibet,* Berkeley: Shambhala, 1970, pp. 147ff.

THE SONNETS TO ORPHEUS

These strange Sonnets were no intended or expected work; they appeared, often *many* in one day (the first part of the book was written in about three days), completely unexpectedly, in February of last year, when I was, moreover, about to gather myself for the continuation of those other poems—the great Duino Elegies. I could do nothing but surrender, purely and obediently, to the dictation of this inner impulse; and I understood only little by little the relation of these verses to the figure of Vera Knoop, who died at the age of eighteen or nineteen, whom I hardly knew and saw only a few times in her life, when she was still a child, though with extraordinary attention and emotion. Without my arranging it this way (except for a few poems at the beginning of the second part, all the Sonnets kept the chronological order of their appearance), it happened that only the next-to-last poems of both parts explicitly refer to Vera, address her, or evoke her figure.

This beautiful child, who had just begun to dance and attracted the attention of everyone who saw her, by the art of movement and transformation which was innate in her body and spirit—unexpectedly declared to her mother that she no longer could or would dance (this happened just at the end of childhood). Her body changed, grew strangely heavy and massive, without losing its beautiful Slavic features; this was already the beginning of the mysterious glandular disease that later was to bring death so quickly. During the time that remained to her, Vera devoted herself to music; finally she only drew—as if the denied dance came forth from her ever more quietly, ever more discreetly.

(To Countess Margot Sizzo-Noris-Crouy, April 12, 1923)

Even to me, in the way they arose and imposed themselves on me, they are perhaps the most mysterious, most enigmatic dictation I have ever endured and achieved; the whole first part was written down in a single breathless obedience.

(To Xaver von Moos, April 20, 1923)

I myself have only now, little by little, comprehended them and found a way to pass them on;—with brief comments that I insert when I read them aloud, I am able to make the whole more intelligible; interconnections are established everywhere, and where a darkness remains, it is the kind of darkness that requires not clarification but surrender. If you ever have questions about any of the poems, I will do my best to answer them.

(To Clara Rilke, April 23, 1923)

There is something in the very nature of these poems [the Elegies and the Sonnets], because they are so condensed and abbreviated (often stating lyric totals, instead of listing the figures necessary for the result), that makes them more easily comprehended by the intuition of those who share their point of view than by what people call "understanding." Two innermost experiences were decisive for their creation: The resolve that grew up more and more, within my deepest feelings, to hold life open toward death; and, on the other hand, my spiritual need to place the transformations of love into this expanded whole, differently from what was possible in the narrower orbit of life (which simply excluded death, as the Other).

This is where the "plot" of these poems might be found, and here and there it stands, I think, simple and strong, in the foreground.

(To Nanny von Escher, December 22, 1923)

During the reading the other night, I thought of you, and wished I could look through this book with you, page by page, in order to present each poem to you in all its power. I know now that there is none that is not clear and productive, even though some are so close to the unsayable mystery that they can't be explained but only—: endured. And I experienced how much my voice, without any conscious effort, contributes to the meaning, if only because the whole miracle through which these verses arose still trembles in it and is transmitted to the listener, with indescribable vibrations.

(To Countess Margot Sizzo-Noris-Crouy, April 12, 1923)

Much in these poems might be difficult to comprehend if one were not familiar with certain assumptions of mine and with my attitude toward love and death; but there is much in them that will open to you completely. . . . My desire to establish this very link with the greatest and most powerful elements in our tradition, my obedience to the inner voice that directed me to set *this* attempt above all others within my work, will help explain to you many passages that seem closed upon first or second glance. Looked at from this perspective, the structure of the whole (unpremeditated, founded entirely within the inner dictation), as well as the parallelisms of the first and second parts, may become more intelligible.

(To Leopold von Schlözer, May 30, 1923)

You are thinking too far beyond the poem when you suppose that you have to bring in the concept of metempsychosis, which is in this sense alien to me. I believe that no poem in the Sonnets to Orpheus has any meaning that is not fully written out in the text, often (it is true) with its most secret names.

(To Countess Margot Sizzo-Noris-Crouy, June 1, 1923)

It can hardly be said to what degree a human being can carry himself over into an artistic concentration as dense as that of the Elegies and of certain Sonnets; often it is uncanny for the person who brought them forth to feel beside him, on the thinner days of life (the many!), *such* an essence of his own being, in its indescribable, ultimate weight. The presence of a poem like this stands out, in the strangest way, above the flatness and insignificance of daily life, and yet precisely out of that daily life was this greater, more valid existence wrested and achieved (how, the achiever himself hardly knows); for hardly has it been done before one again belongs in the general, blinder fate, among those who forget, or know as if they didn't know, and who through an easy vagueness or inexactness help increase the sum of life's mistakes. In this way, every great artistic achievement, even to its furthest possible success, is both a distinction and a humiliation for the one who was capable of it.

(To Countess Mirbach, August 9, 1924)

. . . *we, in the sense of the Elegies, are these transformers of the earth; our entire existence, the flights and plunges of our love, everything, qualifies us for this task* (beside which there is, essentially, no other). (The Sonnets show particular examples of this activity, which appears in them, placed under the name and protection of a dead girl, whose incompletion and innocence holds open the grave-door so that, having passed on, she belongs to those powers which keep the one half of life fresh, and open toward the other, wound-open half.) Elegies and Sonnets support each other constantly—and I consider it an infinite grace that with the same breath I was permitted to fill both these sails: the little rust-colored sail of the Sonnets and the Elegies' gigantic white canvas.

(To Witold Hulewicz, November 13, 1925)

More and more in my life and in my work I am guided by the effort to correct our old repressions, which have removed and gradually estranged from us the mysteries out of whose abundance our lives might become truly infinite. It is true that these mysteries are dreadful, and people have always drawn away from them. But where can we find anything sweet and glorious that would never wear *this* mask, the mask of the dreadful? Life—and we know nothing else— isn't life itself dreadful? But as soon as we acknowledge its dreadfulness (not as opponents: what kind of match could we be for it?), but somehow with a confidence that this very dreadfulness may be something completely *ours,* though something that is just now too great, too vast, too incomprehensible for our learning hearts—: as soon as we accept life's most terrifying dreadfulness, at the risk of perishing from it (i.e., from our own Too-much!)—: then an intuition of blessedness will open up for us and, at this cost, will be ours. Whoever does not, sometime or other, give his full consent, his full and *joyous* consent, to the dreadfulness of life, can never take possession of the unutterable abundance and power of our existence; can only walk on its edge, and one day, when the judgment is given, will have been neither alive nor dead. To show the *identity* of dreadfulness and bliss, these two faces on the same divine head, indeed this one *single* face, which just presents itself this way or that, according to our distance from it or the state of mind in which we perceive it—: this is the true significance and purpose of the Elegies and the Sonnets to Orpheus.

(To Countess Margot Sizzo-Noris-Crouy, April 12, 1923)

I say "sonnets." Though they are the freest, most (as it were) con-
jugated poems that have ever been included under this usually so
motionless and stable form. But precisely this—to conjugate the
sonnet, to intensify it, to give it the greatest possible scope without
destroying it—was for me a strange experiment: which, in any case,
I made no conscious decision to undertake. So strongly was it im-
posed, so fully did it contain its solution in itself.

(To Katharina Kippenberg, February 23, 1922)

Today just one favor more, which I have been wanting to ask of
you for a long time: could you eventually have printed for me one
copy of the "Sonnets to Orpheus," and perhaps also one copy of
the "Elegies," interleaved with blank pages, using paper that can
absorb good ink without making it "bleed"? I would like to append
brief commentaries here and there to the more difficult poems, for
my own use and for the benefit of a few friends; it would be a
curious work, in which I would strangely have to account for the
place of this verse within my own inner proportions. Whether or
not that happens, I would in any case be glad to have both books,
especially the "Sonnets," prepared in this way, so that I can make
notes in it whenever I feel the inclination. (There is no hurry, of
course!)

(To Anton Kippenberg, March 11, 1926)

First Part

I (February 2/5, 1922)

II (February 2/5)

l. 1, *almost a girl:*

Siehe, innerer Mann, dein inneres Mädchen

Look, inner man, at your inner girl

("Turning-point," *The Selected Poetry,* p. 135)

The deepest experience of the creative artist is feminine, for it is an
experience of conceiving and giving birth. The poet Obstfelder once
wrote, speaking of the face of a stranger: "When he began to speak,
it was as though a *woman* had taken a seat within him." It seems to
me that every poet has had that experience in beginning to speak.

(To a young woman, November 20, 1904)

III (FEBRUARY 2/5)

ll. 3f., *crossing / of heart-roads:* "The sanctuaries that stood at cross-roads in classical antiquity were dedicated to sinister deities like Hecate, not to Apollo, the bright god of song." (Hermann Mörchen, *Rilkes Sonette an Orpheus*, Stuttgart: W. Kohlhammer Verlag, 1958, p. 66)

l. 13, *True singing:*

> It is not only the *hearable* in music that is important (something can be pleasant to hear without being *true*). What is decisive for me, in all the arts, is not their outward appearance, not what is called the "beautiful"; but rather their deepest, most inner origin, the buried reality that calls forth their appearance.

(To Princess Marie von Thurn und Taxis-Hohenlohe, November 17, 1912)

l. 14, *A gust inside the god. A wind.:*

> All in a few days, it was a nameless storm, a hurricane in the spirit (like that time at Duino), everything that was fiber and fabric in me cracked.

(Ibid., February 11, 1922, just after the completion of the Elegies)

> Never have I gone through such tremendous gales of being-taken-hold-of: I was an element, Liliane, and could do everything elements can do.

(To Claire Studer-Goll, April 11, 1923)

IV (FEBRUARY 2/5)

V (FEBRUARY 2/5)

l. 5, *It is Orpheus once for all:*

> Ultimately there is only *one* poet, that infinite one who makes himself felt, here and there through the ages, in a mind that can surrender to him.

(To Nanny Wunderly-Volkart, July 29, 1920)

> True art can issue only from a purely anonymous center.

(To R. S., November 22, 1920)

VI (FEBRUARY 2/5)

l. 2, *both realms:*

Engel (sagt man) wüßten oft nicht, ob sie unter
Lebenden gehn oder Toten. Die ewige Strömung

reißt durch beide Bereiche alle Alter
immer mit sich und übertönt sie in beiden.

Angels (they say) don't know whether it is the living
they are moving among, or the dead. The eternal torrent
whirls all ages along in it, through both realms
forever, and their voices are drowned out in its thunderous roar.

(First Duino Elegy, 92ff.)

l. 4, *willow-branch:* From Psalm 137, to Desdemona's song, to modern poetry, the willow has been a symbol of grief. Its association with the dead goes back at least as far as Homer:

But when the North Wind has breathed you across the River of
    Ocean,
you will come to a wooded coast and the Grove of Persephone,
dense with shadowy poplars and willows that shed their seeds.
Beach your boat on that shore as the ocean-tide foams behind you;
then walk ahead by yourself, into the Land of Decay.

(Odyssey X, 508ff.)

Aber erweckten sie uns, die unendlich Toten, ein Gleichnis,
siehe, sie zeigten vielleicht auf die Kätzchen der leeren
Weide, die hängenden, oder
meinten den Regen, der fällt auf dunkles Erdreich im Frühjahr.—

But if the endlessly dead awakened a symbol in us
perhaps they would point to the catkins hanging from the bare
branches of the willow, or
would evoke the raindrops that fall onto the dark earth in springtime.—

(Tenth Elegy, first draft, 106ff.)

l. 10, *earthsmoke and rue:* Herbs used in summoning the dead.

But slowly growing beside it is patience, that delicate "earthsmoke."

(To Gudi Nölke, October 5, 1919)

l. 11, *connection:*

The comprehensible slips away, is transformed; instead of possession one learns connection.

(To Ilse Jahr, February 22, 1923)

VII (FEBRUARY 2/5)

l. 9, *decay in the sepulcher of kings:*

It is true, the gods have neglected no opportunity of exposing us: they let us uncover the great kings of Egypt in their tombs, and we

were able to see them in their natural decay, how they were spared
no indignity. All the utmost achievements of that architecture and
art—led to nothing; behind the fumes of the balsam cake no heaven
lit up, and the loaves and concubines, long turned to clay, had not
apparently been used by any subterranean revelers. Anyone who
considers what an abundance of the purest and most powerful ideas
were here (and continually) rejected and repudiated by the incon-
ceivable beings to whom they had been dedicated: how could he
not tremble for our more exalted future? But he should also con-
sider what the human heart would be if, outside it, anywhere in the
world, certainty existed; final certainty. Suddenly it would lose all
the readiness it had gathered during thousands of years; it would
still be a place that was praiseworthy, but in secret people would
tell of what it had been in former times. For truly, even the greatness
of the gods depends upon their need: upon the fact that, whatever
shrines are kept for them, they are safe nowhere but in our heart.
That is the place they plunge into, out of their sleep, with their still-
unsifted plans, the place where they gather to take counsel, and
where their decree is irresistible.

("The Young Poet," SW 6, 1047f.)

VIII (February 2/5)

IX (February 2/5)

l. 14, *mild:*

I reproach all modern religions for having provided their believers
with consolations and glossings-over of death, instead of giving
them the means of coming to an understanding with it. With it and
with its full, unmasked cruelty: this cruelty is so immense that it is
precisely with *it* that the circle closes; it leads back into a mildness
which is greater, purer, and more perfectly clear (all consolation is
muddy!) than we have ever, even on the sweetest spring day, imag-
ined mildness to be.

(To Countess Margot Sizzo-Noris-Crouy, January 6, 1923)

X (February 2/5)

l. 2, *coffins of stone:* Used as troughs or basins in the fountains of
Italian towns.

Da wurde von den alten Aquädukten
ewiges Wasser in sie eingelenkt . . .

Then, eternal water from the ancient
aqueducts was channeled into them . . .

("Roman Sarcophagi")

l. 5, *those other ones:*

(what is being referred to, after the Roman ones, are those other, uncovered sarcophagi in the famous cemetery of Aliscamps, out of which flowers bloom)

—Rilke's note

l. 6, *shepherd:* See "The Spanish Trilogy," *The Selected Poetry,* pp. 119ff. and 312.

l. 7, *bee-suck nettle: Lamium album,* white dead-nettle.

XI (FEBRUARY 2/5)

l. 1, *"Rider":*

—Hier,
siehe: den *Reiter,* den *Stab,* und das vollere Sternbild
nennen sie: *Fruchtkranz.*

—*Look, there:*
the Rider, *the* Staff, *and the larger constellation*
called Garland of Fruit.

(Tenth Elegy, 90ff.)

XII (FEBRUARY 2/5)

l. 7, *antennas:*

Oh how she [Vera] loved, how she reached out with the antennas of her heart beyond everything that is comprehensible and embrace-able here— . . .

(To Gertrud Ouckama Knoop, January 1922)

XIII (FEBRUARY 2/5)

Comme le fruit se fond en jouissance,
Comme en délice il change son absence
Dans une bouche où sa forme se meurt, . . .

(Valéry, "Le Cimetière Marin")

So wie die Frucht sich auflöst im Genusse,
Abwesenheit Entzücken wird zum Schlusse
in einem Mund, drin ihre Form verschwand, . . .

(Rilke's translation, March 14 and 16, 1921)

l. 9, *"apple"*:

At various times I have had the experience of feeling apples, more than anything else—barely consumed, and often while I was still eating them—being transposed into spirit. Thus perhaps the Fall. (If there *was* one.)

(To Princess Marie von Thurn und Taxis-Hohenlohe, January 16, 1912)

XIV (FEBRUARY 2/5)

XV (FEBRUARY 2/5)

XVI (FEBRUARY 2/5)

One has to know—or guess—that Sonnet XVI is addressed to a dog; I didn't want to add a note to this effect, precisely because I wanted to take him completely into the whole. Any hint would just have isolated him again, singled him out. (This way he takes part down below, belonging and warned, like the dog and the child in Rembrandt's Night Watch.)

(To Clara Rilke, April 23, 1923)

Now it is my turn to thank you, not for Pierrot, for God's sake *no:* it would be his ruin, Pierrot's ruin, the saddest story in the world. How could you even think I might adopt him, what kind of match could I be for his boundless homesickness? Furthermore, apart from the torment of helplessly looking on, I would have the additional torment of sacrificing myself for his sake, which I find especially painful where dogs are involved: they touch me so deeply, these beings who are entirely dependent on us, whom we have helped up to a soul for which there is no heaven. Even though I need all of my heart, it is probable that this would end, end tragically, by my breaking off little pieces from the edge of it at first, then bigger and bigger pieces toward the middle (like dog biscuits) for this Pierrot as he cried for you and no longer understood life; I would, after hesitating for a little while, give up my writing and live entirely for his consolation.

(To N. N., February 8, 1912)

l. 7, *You know the dead:*

"And I was about to (I feel quite cold, Malte, when I think of it), but, God help me, I was just about to say, 'Where is . . .'—when Cavalier shot out from under the table, as he always did, and ran to meet her. I saw it, Malte; I saw it. He ran toward her, although she wasn't coming; for him she *was* coming."

(*The Notebooks of Malte Laurids Brigge,* New York: Random House, 1983, p. 89)

ll. 11f., *don't plant / me inside your heart:*

"In the end a responsibility would arise, which I can't accept. You wouldn't notice how completely you had come to trust me; you would overvalue me and expect from me what I can't perform. You would watch me and approve of everything, even of what is not good. If I want to give you a joy: will I find one? And if one day you are sad and complain to me—will I be able to help you?—And you shouldn't think that *I* am the one who lets you die. Go away, I beg of you: go away."

(*"An Encounter," SW 6, 985)

l. 13, my *master's hand:*

In the poem *to the dog,* by "my master's hand" the hand of the god is meant; here, of "Orpheus." The poet wants to guide this hand so that it too may, for the sake of his [the dog's] infinite sympathy and devotion, bless the dog, who, almost like Esau, has put on his pelt only so that he could share, in his heart, an inheritance that would never come to him: could participate, with sorrow and joy, in all of human existence.

(To Countess Margot Sizzo-Noris-Crouy, June 1, 1923)

XVII (FEBRUARY 2/5)

XVIII (FEBRUARY 2/5)

l. 14, *remain:*

"You see, I want to be usable to God just the way I am. What I do here, my work, I want to keep doing it toward him, without having my stream interrupted, if I can express it like that, not even in Christ, who was once the water for many. The machine, for example —I can't explain it to him, he doesn't grasp it. I know you won't laugh if I say this so simply, it's the best way. God, though: I have a feeling I can bring it to *him,* my machine and its firstborn, or even my whole work, it enters him without any trouble. Just as it was easy once for the shepherds to bring the gods of their life a lamb or a vegetable-basket or the most beautiful bunch of grapes."

(*"The Young Workman's Letter," SW 6, 1126)

XIX (FEBRUARY 2/5)

XX (FEBRUARY 2/5)

And imagine, one thing *more,* in another connection (in the "Sonnets to Orpheus," twenty-five sonnets, written, suddenly, in the prestorm, as a monument for Vera Knoop), I wrote, *made,* the *horse,* you know, the free happy white horse with the hobble on his foot,

who once, as evening fell, on a Volga meadow, came bounding
toward us at a gallop—:

how

I made him, as an "ex-voto" for Orpheus!—What is time?—*When*
is Now? Across so many years he bounded, with his absolute hap-
piness, into my wide-open feeling.

(To Lou Andreas-Salomé, February 11, 1922)

There is also an account of the incident in Lou Andreas-Salomé's
travel diary:

As we were standing by the Volga, a neigh resounded through the
silent evening, and a frisky little horse, having finished its day of
work, came quickly trotting toward the herd, which was spending
the night somewhere, far away, in the meadow-steppes. In the dis-
tance one could now and then see the shepherds' fire blazing in the
clear night. After a while a second little horse, from somewhere else,
followed, more laboriously: they had tied a wooden hobble to one
of his legs, in order to stop him from wildly leaping into the wheat-
field.

(*Briefwechsel*, p. 611)

l. 13, *cycle of myths:*

It is done, *done!* / The blood- and myth-cycle of ten (ten!) strange
years has been completed.—It was (now for the first time I feel it
entirely) like a mutilation of my heart, that this did not exist. And
now it is here.

(To Nanny Wunderly-Volkart, February 10, 1922)

XXI (FEBRUARY 9; inserted here as a replacement for the original
I,21; see Appendix, pp. 134–35)

The little spring-song seems to me, as it were, an "interpretation" of
a remarkable, dancing music that I once heard sung by the convent
children at a morning Mass in the little church at Ronda (in southern
Spain). The children, who kept leaping to a dance rhythm, sang a
text I didn't know, to the accompaniment of triangle and tambou-
rine.

—Rilke's note*

If the Sonnets to Orpheus were allowed to reach publication, prob-
ably two or three of them, which, I now see, just served as

---

* This and the note to II,11 are the only two notes Rilke himself ever
published. The others marked "Rilke's note" were handwritten in a copy of
the Sonnets which he sent to Herr and Frau Leopold von Schlözer on May
30, 1923.

conduits for the stream (e.g. the XXIst) and after its passage-through remained empty, would have to be replaced by others.

(To Gertrud Ouckama Knoop, February 7, 1922)

It makes me uncomfortable to think of that XXIst poem, the "empty" one in which the "transmissions" appear ("The New, my friends, is not a matter of") . . . , please paste it over, right now, with this child's-spring-song, written today, which, I think, enriches the sound of the whole cycle and stands fairly well, as a pendant, opposite the white horse.

This little song, which had risen into my consciousness when I woke up this morning, fully formed up to the eighth line, and the rest of it immediately afterward, appears to me like an interpretation of a "Mass"—a real *Mass,* gaily accompanied as if with hanging garlands of sound: the convent children sang it to I don't know what text, but in this dance-step, in the little nuns'-church at Ronda (in southern Spain—); sang it, one can hear, to tambourine and triangle!—It fits, doesn't it, into these interrelationships of the Sonnets to Orpheus: as the brightest spring-tone in them? (I think it does.)

(Does the paper more-or-less match? I hope it is the same.)

Only this—and only because that XXIst is like a blot on my conscience.

(To Gertrud Ouckama Knoop, February 9, 1922)

XXII (FEBRUARY 2/5)

XXIII (FEBRUARY 13)

This Sonnet I have—at least temporarily—inserted as the XXIII, so that what has become the *first* part of the Sonnets now contains twenty-six poems.

(To Gertrud Ouckama Knoop, March 18, 1922)

XXIV (FEBRUARY 2/5)

XXV (FEBRUARY 2/5)

(to Vera)

—Rilke's note

XXVI (FEBRUARY 2/5)

l. 2, *rejected:*

Three years went by, but Orpheus still refused
to love another woman: so intense
his grief was, for his lost Eurydice;

or else because he had vowed to stay alone.
But many women desired him, and raged
at his abrupt rejection.

(Ovid, Metamorphoses X, 78ff.)

l. 2, *attacked:*

From a nearby hill the frenzied women, bristling
in skins of savage beasts, at last caught sight
of Orpheus, as he sat absorbed in music,
accompanied by the sweet lyre. One of them,
her long hair streaming in the wind, cried out:
"Look! there he is, that man who shows us such
contempt." And, with a yell, she hurled her spear
straight at the singing mouth . . .

(Ibid. XI, 3ff.)

l. 5, *could not destroy your head or your lyre:*

His limbs lay scattered; but the river Hebrus
took the head and lyre, and as they floated
down its stream, the lyre began to play
a mournful tune, and the lifeless tongue sang out
mournfully, and both the river-banks
answered, with their own, faint, mournful echo.

(Ibid. XI, 50ff.)

l. 7, *stones:*

Another threw a stone; but in mid-flight,
overwhelmed by the beauty of the song,
it fell at his feet, as though to beg forgiveness
for its violent intention.

(Ibid. XI, 10ff.)

l. 9, *At last they killed you:*

Such music would have moved to softness all
these stones and spears; except that the wild shrieking,
shrill flutes, the blare of trumpets, drumbeats, howls
of the enraged bacchantes had completely
drowned out the lyre's voice. Until at last
the unhearing stones reddened with poet's blood.

(Ibid. XI, 15ff.)

l. 14, *a rescuing voice:*

> —Und diese, von Hingang
> lebenden Dinge verstehn, daß du sie rühmst; vergänglich,
> traun sie ein Rettendes uns, den Vergänglichsten, zu.

—And these Things, / which live by perishing, understand that you are praising them; transient, / they believe that we are capable of rescuing them—we, the most transient of all.

(Ninth Elegy, 63ff.)

Second Part

I (Approximately FEBRUARY 23; the last of the Sonnets to be written)

II (FEBRUARY 15/17)

III (FEBRUARY 15/17)

l. 7, *sixteen-pointer:* A large stag, with sixteen points or branches to its antlers.

IV (FEBRUARY 15/17)

> Any "allusion," I am convinced, would contradict the indescribable *presence* of the poem. So in the unicorn no parallel with Christ is intended; rather, all love of the non-proven, the non-graspable, all belief in the value and reality of whatever our heart has through the centuries created and lifted up out of itself: that is what is praised in this creature. . . . The unicorn has ancient associations with virginity, which were continually honored during the Middle Ages. Therefore this Sonnet states that, though it is nonexistent for the profane, it comes into being as soon as it appears in the "mirror" which the virgin holds up in front of it (see the tapestries of the 15th century) and "in her," as in a second mirror that is just as pure, just as mysterious.

(To Countess Margot Sizzo-Noris-Crouy, June 1, 1923)

V (FEBRUARY 15; chronologically the first poem of the Second Part)

l. 7, so *overpowered with abundance:*

> I am like the little anemone I once saw in the garden in Rome: it had opened so wide during the day that it could no longer close at night. It was terrifying to see it in the dark meadow, wide open,

still taking everything in, into its calyx, which seemed as if it had been furiously torn back, with the much too vast night above it. And alongside, all its prudent sisters, each one closed around its small measure of profusion.

(To Lou Andreas-Salomé, June 26, 1914)

VI (FEBRUARY 15)

the rose of antiquity was a simple "eglantine," red and yellow, in the colors that appear in flame. It blooms here, in the Valais, in certain gardens.

—Rilke's note

Every day, as I contemplate these admirable white roses, I wonder whether they aren't the most perfect image of that unity—I would even say, that identity—of absence and presence which perhaps constitutes the fundamental equation of our life.

(To Madame M.-R., January 4, 1923)

VII (FEBRUARY 15/17)

By the brook I picked marsh-marigolds, almost green, a bit of quite fresh yellow painted into the calyx at the last moment. Inside, around the stamens, an oil-soaked circle, as if they had eaten butter. Green smell from the tubelike stems. Then to find it left behind on my hand, closely related through it. Girl friends, long ago in child-hood, with their hot hands: was it this that so moved me?

(Spanish Notebook, 1913; quoted in *Rilke und Benvenuta*, Wien: W. Andermann, 1943, p. 157)

VIII (FEBRUARY 15/17)

l. 4, *the lamb with the talking scroll:*

The lamb (in medieval paintings) which speaks only by means of a scroll with an inscription on it.

—Rilke's note

Dedication, *Egon von Rilke* (1873–1880): Youngest child of Rilke's father's brother.

I think of him often and keep returning to his image, which has remained indescribably moving to me. So much "childhood"—the sad and helpless side of childhood—is embodied for me in his form, in the ruff he wore, his little neck, his chin, his beautiful disfigured eyes. So I evoked him once more in connection with that eighth sonnet, which expresses transience, after he had already served, in

the Notebooks of Malte Laurids Brigge, as the model for little Erik
Brahe, who died in childhood.

(To Phia Rilke, January 24, 1924; in Carl Sieber,
René Rilke: Die Jugend Rainer Maria Rilkes,
Leipzig: Insel Verlag, 1932, pp. 59f.)

IX (FEBRUARY 15/17)

l. 9, *true mercy:* See note to I,9 (*Milde* can mean either "mildness" or
"mercy").

X (FEBRUARY 15/17)

XI (FEBRUARY 15/17)

Refers to the way in which, according to an ancient hunting-custom
in certain regions of Karst, the strangely pale grotto-doves are
caught. Hunters carefully lower large pieces of cloth into the caverns
and then suddenly shake them. The doves, frightened out, are shot
during their terrified escape.

—Rilke's note

Meanwhile I went along on a dove-hunting expedition to one of
the Karst grottos, quietly eating juniper berries while the hunters
forgot me in their concentration on the beautiful wild doves flying
with loud wingbeats out of the caves.

(To Katharina Kippenberg, October 31, 1911)

l. 4, *Karst:* A region along the Dalmatian coast (north of Trieste and
not far from Duino Castle) known for its limestone caverns.

l. 9, *pity:*

On our way home, as if to answer all these unresolved questions
about human life, Rilke repeated to me an old Indian legend.

"By the seashore lived three old monks. They were so wise and
holy that every day a small miracle happened for them: when they
had finished their morning devotions and gone to bathe, they hung
their robes on the wind; and the robes stayed there, floating in the
wind, until the old men came back to get them.

"One day as they were bathing, they saw a large eagle fly over the
sea. Suddenly it swooped down into the water, and when it flew up
again it had a struggling fish in its beak. One of the monks said,
'Wicked bird!'—Upon which his robe fell to the ground and lay
there.

"The second monk said, 'You poor fish!' And his robe, also, fell
to the ground and lay there.

"The third monk looked at the bird as it flew off with the fish in its beak, and watched it grow smaller and smaller and finally disappear into the morning light. The monk said nothing—and *his* robe remained hanging in the wind."

(Reported by Magda von Hattingberg, *Rilke und Benvenuta,* p. 137)

XII (FEBRUARY 15/17)

l. 13, *Daphne:* A nymph pursued by Apollo and transformed into a laurel. See Ovid, Metamorphoses I, 452ff.

XIII (FEBRUARY 15/17)

In a letter telling Vera's mother about the unexpected appearance of the second part of the Sonnets, Rilke wrote:

Today I am sending you only *one* of these sonnets, because, of the entire cycle, it is the one that is closest to me and ultimately the one that is the most valid.

(To Gertrud Ouckama Knoop, March 18, 1922)

The thirteenth sonnet of the second part is for me the most valid of all. It includes all the others, and it expresses *that* which—though it still far exceeds me—my purest, most final achievement would someday, in the midst of life, have to be.

(To Katharina Kippenberg, April 2, 1922)

l. 14, *cancel the count:*

Renunciation of love or fulfillment in love: *both* are wonderful and beyond compare only where the entire love-experience, with *all* its barely differentiable ecstasies, is allowed to occupy a central position: there (in the rapture of a few lovers or saints of *all* times and *all* religions) renunciation and completion are identical. Where the infinite *wholly* enters (whether as minus or plus), the ah so human number drops away, as the road that has now been completely traveled—and what remains is the having arrived, *the being!*

(To Rudolf Bodländer, March 23, 1922)

XIV (FEBRUARY 15/17)

XV (FEBRUARY 17)

XVI (FEBRUARY 17/19)

XVII (FEBRUARY 17/19)

XVIII (FEBRUARY 17/19)

XIX (FEBRUARY 17/23)

l. 13, *understand it and praise it:*

To want to improve the situation of another human being presupposes an insight into his circumstances such as not even a poet has toward a character he himself has created. How much less insight is there in the so infinitely excluded helper, whose scatteredness becomes complete with his gift. Wanting to change or improve someone's situation means offering him, in exchange for difficulties in which he is practiced and experienced, other difficulties that will find him perhaps even more bewildered. If at any time I was able to pour out into the mold of my heart the imaginary voices of the dwarf or the beggar, the metal of this cast was not obtained from any wish that the dwarf or the beggar might have a less difficult time. On the contrary: only through a praising of their incomparable fate could the poet, with his full attention suddenly given to them, be true and fundamental, and there is nothing that he would have to fear and refuse so much as a corrected world in which the dwarfs are stretched out and the beggars enriched. The God of completeness sees to it that these varieties do not cease, and it would be a most superficial attitude to consider the poet's joy in this suffering multiplicity as an esthetic pretense.

(To Hermann Pongs, October 21, 1924)

XX (FEBRUARY 17/23)

l. 5, *Fate:*

What we call fate does not come into us from the outside, but emerges *from* us.

(To Franz Xaver Kappus, August 12, 1904)

l. 10, *fish:*

. . . I sank, weighted down with a millstone's torpor, to the bottom of silence, below the fish, who only at times pucker their mouths into a discreet Oh, which is inaudible.

(To Princess Marie von Thurn und Taxis-Hohenlohe, January 14, 1913)

l. 13, *a place:*

Jacobsen once wrote how annoyed he was that his remarkable short novel had to be called "Two Worlds"; again and again he had felt compelled to say: "Two World." In the same way, it often happens that one is at odds with the outward behavior of language and wants something inside it, an innermost language, a language of word-kernels, a language which is not plucked from stems, up above, but gathered as language-seeds—wouldn't the perfect hymn to the sun be composed in this language, and isn't the pure silence of love like heart-soil around such language-kernels? Ah, how often one wishes to speak a few levels deeper; my prose in "Proposal for an Experiment" ["Primal Sound"] lies deeper, gets a bit farther into the essential, than the prose of the *Malte*, but one penetrates such a very little way down, one remains with just an intuition of what kind of speech is possible in the place where silence is.

(To Nanny Wunderly-Volkart, February 4, 1920)

XXI (February 17/23)

l. 3, *Ispahan* (mod., Isfahan) *or Shiraz:* Persian cities famous for their magnificent gardens. Shiraz also contains the tombs of the poets Hafiz and S'adi.

XXII (February 17/23)

l. 5, *bell:*

For me it was Easter just once; that was during the long, excited, extraordinary night when, with the whole populace crowding around, the bells of Ivan Veliky crashed into me in the darkness, one after another. That was my Easter, and I think it is huge enough for a whole lifetime. . . .

(To Lou Andreas-Salomé, March 31, 1904)

l. 7, *Karnak:* Rilke spent two months in Egypt early in 1911 and was profoundly moved by

that incomprehensible temple-world of Karnak, which, the very first evening, and again yesterday, under a moon just beginning to wane, I saw, saw, saw—my God, you pull yourself together, and with all your might you try to believe your two focused eyes—and yet it begins above them, reaches out everywhere above and beyond them (only a god can cultivate such a field of vision)—a calyx column stands there, alone, a survivor, and you can't encompass it, so far out beyond your life does it reach; only together with the night can you somehow take it in, perceiving it with the stars, as a whole, and then for a second it becomes human—a human experience.

(To Clara Rilke, January 18, 1911)

XXIII (February 17/23)
(to the reader)

—Rilke's note

l. 3, *a dog's imploring glance:*

Alas, I have not completely gotten over expecting the "nouvelle opération" to come from some human intervention; and yet, what's the use, since it is my lot to pass the human by, as it were, and arrive at the extreme limit, the edge of the earth, as recently in Cordova, when an ugly little bitch, in the last stage of pregnancy, came up to me. She was not a remarkable animal, was full of accidental puppies over whom no great fuss would be made; but since we were all alone, she came over to me, hard as it was for her, and raised her eyes enlarged by trouble and inwardness and sought my glance— and in her own way was truly everything that goes beyond the individual, to I don't know where, into the future or into the incomprehensible. The situation ended in her getting a lump of sugar from my coffee, but incidentally, oh so incidentally, we read Mass together, so to speak; in itself, the action was nothing but giving and receiving, yet the sense and the seriousness and our whole silent understanding was beyond all bounds.

(To Princess Marie von Thurn und Taxis-Hohenlohe, December 17, 1912)

XXIV (FEBRUARY 19/23)

l. 5, *Gods:*

Does it confuse you that I say God and gods and, for the sake of completeness, haunt you with these dogmatic words (as with a ghost), thinking that they will have some kind of meaning for you also? But grant, for a moment, that there is a realm beyond the senses. Let us agree that from his earliest beginnings man has created gods in whom just the deadly and menacing and destructive and terrifying elements in life were contained—its violence, its fury, its impersonal bewilderment—all tied together into one thick knot of malevolence: something alien to us, if you wish, but something which let us admit that we were aware of it, endured it, even acknowledged it for the sake of a sure, mysterious relationship and inclusion in it. For *we were this too;* only we didn't know what to do with this side of our experience; it was too large, too dangerous, too many-sided, it grew above and beyond us, into an excess of meaning; we found it impossible (what with the many demands of a life adapted to habit and achievement) to deal with these unwieldly and ungraspable forces; and so we agreed to place them outside us.—But since they were an overflow of our own being, its most powerful element, indeed were *too* powerful, were huge, violent, incomprehensible, often monstrous—: how could they not, concentrated in one place, exert an influence and ascendancy over us? And, remember, from the outside now. Couldn't the history of God be treated as an almost never-explored area of the human soul,

one that has always been postponed, saved, and finally ne-
glected . . . ?

And then, you see, the same thing happened with death. Experi-
enced, yet not to be fully experienced by us in its reality, continually
overshadowing us yet never truly acknowledged, forever violating
and surpassing the meaning of life—it too was banished and ex-
pelled, so that it might not constantly interrupt us in the search for
this meaning. Death, which is probably so close to us that the
distance between it and the life-center inside us cannot be measured,
now became something external, held farther away from us every
day, a presence that lurked somewhere in the void, ready to pounce
upon this person or that in its evil choice. More and more, the
suspicion grew up against death that it was the contradiction, the
adversary, the invisible opposite in the air, the force that makes all
our joys wither, the perilous glass of our happiness, out of which
we may be spilled at any moment. . . .

All this might still have made a kind of sense if we had been able
to keep God and death at a distance, as mere ideas in the realm of
the mind—: but Nature knew nothing of this banishment that we
had somehow accomplished—when a tree blossoms, death as well
as life blossoms in it, and the field is full of death, which from its
reclining face sends forth a rich expression of life, and the animals
move patiently from one to the other—and everywhere around us,
death is at home, and it watches us out of the cracks in Things, and
a rusty nail that sticks out of a plank somewhere, does nothing day
and night except rejoice over death.

(To Lotte Hepner, November 8, 1915)

XXV (FEBRUARY 19/23)

(Companion-piece to the first spring-song of the children in the First
Part of the Sonnets)

—Rilke's note

XXVI (FEBRUARY 19/23)

XXVII (FEBRUARY 19/23)

l. 4, *Demiurge:* In the Gnostic tradition, a lower deity who created
the world of time.

XXVIII (FEBRUARY 19/23)
(to Vera)

—Rilke's note

XXIX (FEBRUARY 19/23)
(to a friend of Vera's)

—Rilke's note

l. 3, *like a bell:*

With this bell tower the little island, in all its fervor, is attached to the past; the tower fixes the dates and dissolves them again, because ever since it was built it has been ringing out time and destiny over the lake, as though it included in itself the visibility of all the lives that have been surrendered here; as though again and again it were sending their transitoriness into space, invisibly, in the sonorous transformations of its notes.

(To Countess Aline Dietrichstein, June 26, 1917)

l. 4, *What feeds upon your face:*

O und die Nacht, die Nacht, wenn der Wind voller Weltraum
uns am Angesicht zehrt—

Oh and the night, the night, when the wind full of cosmic space / feeds upon our face—

(First Elegy, 18f.)

Atme das Dunkel der Erde und wieder
aufschau! Wieder. Leicht und gesichtlos
lehnt sich von oben Tiefe dir an. Das gelöste
nachtenthaltene Gesicht giebt dem deinigen Raum.

*Breathe-in the darkness of earth and again
look up! Again. Airy and faceless,
from above, the depths bend toward you. The face that is dissolved
and contained in the night will give more space to your own.*

(SW 2, 54)

l. 10, *in their magic ring:*

[The poet's] is a naïve, aeolian soul, which is not ashamed to dwell where the senses intersect [*sich kreuzen*], and which lacks nothing, because these unfolded senses form a ring in which there are no gaps . . .

("The Books of a Woman in Love," SW 6, 1018)

APPENDIX

My dear, hardly had Strohl sent me back the little book with the 25 Orpheus Sonnets when this thread proceeded further, into a new fabric—a quantity of additional Sonnets have arisen these past few days, perhaps fifteen or more, but I won't keep them all—I am now so rich that I can afford to *choose!* What a world of grace we live in, after all! What powers are waiting to fill us, constantly shaken vessels that we are. We think we are under one kind of "guidance"— but they are already at work *inside* us. The only thing that belongs to us, as completely ours, is patience; but what immense capital that is—and what interest it bears in its time!—Consolation enough for eighthundredthirtyseven lives of average length.

(To Nanny Wunderly-Volkart, February 18, 1922)

[I] (Approximately FEBRUARY 3; first version of I,7)

And I would appreciate it if you could *replace* the VIIth Sonnet with the enclosed variant (just the first stanza of the previous version remains—the rest always embarrassed me by its exaggerated pathos, and I have long since crossed it out).

(To Gertrud Ouckama Knoop, March 18, 1922)

l. 14, *Golden Fleece:* In some versions of the myth, Orpheus accompanied Jason and the Argonauts on their voyage.

[II] (FEBRUARY 2/5; originally I,21)

[III] (FEBRUARY 15/17)

[IV] (FEBRUARY 15/17)

l. 1, *stela:*

Erstaunte euch nicht auf attischen Stelen die Vorsicht
menschlicher Geste? war nicht Liebe und Abschied
so leicht auf die Schultern gelegt, als wär es aus anderm
Stoffe gemacht als bei uns? Gedenkt euch der Hände,
wie sie drucklos beruhen, obwohl in den Torsen die Kraft steht.
Diese Beherrschten wußten damit: so weit sind wirs,
dieses ist unser, uns *so* zu berühren; stärker
stemmen die Götter uns an. Doch dies ist Sache der Götter.

Weren't you astonished by the caution of human gestures
on Attic stelas? Wasn't love-and-departure
placed so gently on shoulders that it seemed to be made
of a different substance than in our world? Remember the hands,
how weightlessly they rest, though there is power in the torsos.
These self-mastered figures know: "We can go this far,
this is ours, to touch one another this lightly; the gods
can press down harder upon us. But that is the gods' affair."

(Second Elegy, 66ff.)

See also *The Selected Poetry,* p. 321.

[V] (FEBRUARY 16/17)

This Sonnet probably refers to Goethe, who at the age of seventy-four fell in love with the nineteen-year-old Ulrike von Levetzow.

l. 9, *Hymen:* Greek god of marriage, usually depicted as a handsome young man crowned with a wreath and holding a wedding-torch.

l. 12, *laments:* Goethe commemorated his love in a poem known as the Marienbad Elegy.

[VI] (FEBRUARY 16/17)

l. 3, *Villa d'Este:* Italian Renaissance palace near Tivoli, famous for its fountains and terraced gardens.

[VII] (FEBRUARY 16/17)

[VIII] (FEBRUARY 17/19)

[IX] (Approximately FEBRUARY 23)

FRAGMENTS

[i] (Approximately FEBRUARY 3; written between I,8 and I,9)

[ii] (Approximately FEBRUARY 3; related to I,11)

[iii] (Approximately FEBRUARY 4; written between I,17 and I,18)

[iv] (FEBRUARY 12 or 13; draft of II,2)

[v] (FEBRUARY 16/17)

[vi] (FEBRUARY 16/17)

[vii] (FEBRUARY 17/19)

[viii] (FEBRUARY 19/23; draft of II,25)

[ix] (FEBRUARY 19/23)

[x] (Approximately FEBRUARY 23)

[xi] (Approximately FEBRUARY 23)

ACKNOWLEDGMENTS

I would like to express my gratitude to Chana Bloch, Robert Pinsky, Alan Williamson, and John Herman, my editor, for their many helpful suggestions.

I am also grateful to the Ingram Merrill Foundation for an award that helped pay the bills while I was working on this book.

ABOUT THE TRANSLATOR

Stephen Mitchell was born in Brooklyn, New York, in 1943 and studied at Amherst, the University of Paris, and Yale. His previous books include *Dropping Ashes on the Buddha: The Teaching of Zen Master Seung Sahn* (Grove Press, 1976); *Into the Whirlwind: A Translation of the Book of Job* (Doubleday, 1979); and *The Selected Poetry of Rainer Maria Rilke* (Random House, 1982). He lives with his wife, Vicki Chang, an acupuncturist and healer, in Berkeley, California.